'I became a social worker because I believ
helping, creativity, intellectual endeavour and action for social change came
together. Where social science meets art meets interpersonal practice, with a
whole lot of rights in the mix. This book tells me I was, and am, not alone and
that social work with adults is re-finding its roots, its identity and its future.

This compelling collection of stories of our profession is written with verve.
It leaves bureaucratic, timid, constrained and managerialist approaches for
dust. This is social work via Patti Smith, Paulo Freire and Ken Loach. Committed,
empowering, liberating, creative.

The authors know all about the impact of austerity and welfare reform. In
the context of this destruction and harm in public service resourcing they ask
vital questions – how different do things need to be to create humane support
that people actually value and which advances their rights? How corroded have
relationships become between citizens and public servants under marketised
and transactional care management? And how do we take responsibility as
social workers for changing what we do and how we are valued in the families
and communities we serve?

The ideals of social work are discussed with passion and grounded in real
life and real social work decisions.

It's a brave book too – uncompromising and critical. If some people's noses
aren't out of joint, it won't have done its job. It has and they will be. Well done
to the authors for creating something fresh and important.'

– Dr Ruth Allen, CEO of the
British Association of Social Workers

Love, hope and the messy stuff, stories of social work with adults. The book
gives examples of practice making links to social work approaches, legislation
and case law, reflecting on the reality of adult social work based on the rights
of the person. A valuable insight into practice for social workers and social
work students.'

– Karen Maude, Practice Educator of the Year
2018, Social Worker of the Year Awards

'This book shares stories that show how people's lives have been transformed through getting to know people. Whether you're a social work professional, support worker or gobby punk activist (like us), this book demonstrates the importance of upholding everyone's human rights. This collection of practical stories isn't just for social workers, anyone working in social care will be able to draw and reflect on them to check we're doing everything we can to uphold the human rights of the people we work with. At our charity we view ourselves as gobby punk activists and we have no social work background. To read that our work has partly inspired this book is a thrill because it reminds us that we all have a part to play in upholding everyone's human rights. This book gives positive, practical stories of how relationship-based social work can make a huge difference to individual's lives. It begs the question "if we don't have the time to make sure the people we support are happy in their life, are we prepared to risk-assess their life full of misery?"'

– *Paul Richards, Director, Stay Up Late*

'I would have bought this book for the title alone, but the content is dazzling. Written by social workers who clearly love their work, it is powerful, hopeful, funny, informed and based on years of experience and learning. Social care is in need of an injection of colour, love, fun, innovation and creativity. *Social Work, Cats and Rocket Science* is a cracking start.'

– *Sara Ryan, mum to Connor Sparrowhawk,*
author of Justice for Laughing Boy

'Whether a politician, a policy maker, a practitioner or a member of the public, everyone should read this. A collection of essays which beautifully portrays the role of social work in society. Much misunderstood, social work walks the tightrope of rights and responsibilities, autonomy and protection, care and control. An illuminating and passionate account of social work in the 21st century.'

– *Isabelle Trowler, Chief Social Worker*
for England (Children & Families)

Social Work, Cats and Rocket Science

of related interest

The Straightforward Guide to Safeguarding Adults
From Getting the Basics Right to Applying the Care Act and Criminal Investigations
Deborah Barnett
ISBN 978 1 78592 327 2
eISBN 978 1 78450 640 7

Supporting Older People Using Attachment-Informed and Strengths-Based Approaches
Imogen Blood and Lydia Guthrie
ISBN 978 1 78592 123 0
eISBN 978 1 78450 387 1

Safeguarding Adults Under the Care Act 2014
Understanding Good Practice
Edited by Adi Cooper OBE and Emily White
Foreword by Lyn Romeo
ISBN 978 1 78592 094 3
eISBN 978 1 78450 358 1
Part of the Knowledge in Practice *series*

Care Act 2014
An A-Z of Law and Practice
Michael Mandelstam
ISBN 978 1 84905 559 8
eISBN 978 0 85700 991 3

Using Solution Focused Practice with Adults in Health and Social Care
Judith Milner and Steve Myers
ISBN 978 1 78592 067 7
eISBN 978 1 78450 325 3

The Survival Guide for Newly Qualified Social Workers in Adult and Mental Health Services
Hitting the Ground Running
Diane Galpin, Jenny Bigmore and Jo Parker
ISBN 978 1 84905 158 3
eISBN 978 0 85700 557 1

SOCIAL WORK, CATS AND ROCKET SCIENCE

STORIES OF MAKING A DIFFERENCE IN SOCIAL WORK WITH ADULTS

ELAINE JAMES, ROB MITCHELL AND HANNAH MORGAN

WITH MARK HARVEY AND IAN BURGESS

Forewords by Lyn Romeo and Mark Neary

Jessica Kingsley *Publishers*
London and Philadelphia

First published in 2020
by Jessica Kingsley Publishers
73 Collier Street
London N1 9BE, UK
and
400 Market Street, Suite 400
Philadelphia, PA 19106, USA

www.jkp.com

Library of Congress Cataloging in Publication Data
A CIP catalog record for this book is available from the Library of Congress

British Library Cataloguing in Publication Data
A CIP catalogue record for this book is available from the British Library

ISBN 978 1 78592 519 1
eISBN 978 1 78450 985 9

Printed and bound in Great Britain

Contents

Foreword

Over the last few years I have noticed a subtle but emergent movement. A ground swell of new and divergent thinking, ideas, art and creativity, all starting to shape a new wave of social work activism, practice and partnership with citizens. Social media has been a core part of this movement, connecting people, ideas and debates about social work across the country and indeed, the world. Never before have we had the opportunity to discuss, learn and share as we have now. The rules of learning and critically reflective practice are being enhanced everyday by these new connections and opportunities.

Within this space, the creators of this book have contributed considerable material and thinking. Reflective and honest, their style has incorporated not just social work values, thinking and research but also art, music and popular culture, helping to shape a message that is often difficult to hear. An explicit and unequivocal commitment to challenging the power in the hands of social work is core to their message. People should hold this power and social work should be there to support and serve.

Like the pamphlet movements of the 19th century that shaped political ideas, challenged oppression and inequality, we have seen the rise of the blog – the modern equivalent of the pamphlet, reaching far and wide, stirring debate and more importantly calling for change and new solutions. This book harnesses the power of the blog as written by these authors. This collection extends the thinking from their original blogs and seeks to consider the response a social worker may take in similar situations, using critical reflection and self-awareness as core. In a world where social media can be a force of negativity including in social work. You will find these contributors will offer critique in a fair and powerful way but never without solution and certainly never without hope.

I have had the opportunity to work closely with all of the contributors to this book over the last five years. Individually they have helped shape these new movements and create some in their own inimitable style. As a group, they have led organisations and projects both nationally and locally, from the Adult Principal Social Work network through to research and storytelling, adding to the collective knowledge of the profession and health and social care as a whole. They are also not afraid to challenge national thinking or prominent social care organisations, arranging fringe events alongside citizens, writing articles and sharing videos to challenge the narrow thinking that can still permeate our social care systems.

This book will introduce you to something new and thought provoking. The stories and ideas embedded in the chapters are diverse and challenging. They will introduce the importance of love and sex to your practice as well as radios, balloons, dancing, music and many other wonderful and sad scenarios.

You may wonder how cats and rocket science have a role in a book about social work. Well, cats are core to some of these stories and highlight the need for practitioners to think beyond the presenting crisis or perception of help that we may feel the urge to prescribe. But rocket science is more personal, a metaphor for the new world of social media and technology shaping our profession and people's lives. An understanding that the complexity of human lives and relationships is far more complicated than the inner workings of a rocket ship, yet in many ways much simpler and more beautiful. For some the powerful words in the song *Rocket Science* by Mary Cigarettes resonates personally and powerfully, reflecting the heart of this book.

This book is all about you embracing new thinking and using points of reference in your practice that go way beyond the norm. You can read this book and take so many things from it – new thinking around practice, personal reflection, laughter and, probably, tears. But more importantly what you will feel is a solid commitment to social justice and the human rights of some of the most discriminated and oppressed members of our society, with a dash of love, science, a tweet or two and a great sound track. The new social work bohemians can be found inside.

Lyn Romeo, Chief Social Worker for Adults (England)
at the Department of Health and Social Care

Foreword

Social services entered our life in 1988. My wife and I were in a maternity ward. The 32-week scan had revealed that our daughter had died in the womb and Julie had just been through a six-hour labour with us knowing that the outcome would be a short time cradling our dead child. It was grim. We were in a single room but could still hear the sounds coming from the ward next door. Into this horror scene walked Angela the social worker. Snowy white hair, A-line tartan skirt and sensible brogues, she had the look of a kindly Miss Marple about her. She was mumsy but mumsy was exactly what we needed at that time. That first meeting was very short and discreet but Angela stayed around for the next two years until her retirement. I had nobody else to compare her with but my instinct told me that she was definitely old school. She helped us arrange a memorial service for our baby and she offered wise but gentle counselling. After my wife had a breakdown, Angela turned up with Marmite® sandwiches in case I wasn't eating properly. By 1990 she'd retired but we had one final, emotional encounter with her in 1995, seven years after that first meeting. We'd had Steven for two weeks after the adoption and took him to our local church's summer fete. And there she was, serving the Robinsons Barley Water®. We had a group hug, shed a few years and she made Steven a bacon sandwich. The habits of a lifetime's service.

By 1993, we'd met Seona the social worker. She was allocated to assess us as potential adoptive parents. I think she liked us and saw that we might have something to offer but she was tough. Originally from the North East, she didn't pull her punches but that was cool because we always knew where we stood with her. We found out we'd passed the approval panel on the day we buried my father in law. Seona knew about the funeral and didn't want to intrude but turned up at 7 p.m. in the evening to break the good news at the end of a very sad day. Then came the interminable 'matching' process but Seona fought our corner and eventually, one summer day in 1995, she drove us back from Lincolnshire with Steven sitting next to me on the back seat. Her job done, we were handed over to a 'post-placement' colleague, but I'll never forget our final meeting. A popular TV drama at the time was *Our Friends in The North* and because of her roots, Seona was a big fan. The final episode had aired the night before and we both wept buckets as we recalled the last scene of Daniel Craig crossing the Tyne bridge battered and bruised by life. Fast forward 22 years and I was speaking at a conference in Northampton. I was sitting outside having a pre-talk cigarette when I heard, 'Mark!' and Seona came sprinting across the lawn. After the event, she went miles out of her way and drove me all the way to my front door in echoes of that Lincolnshire car journey all those years earlier.

That was it with social workers for the next few years. Then, when Steven was about 14, I was offered some teaching work two evenings a week so we asked for support for Julie whilst I was out working. Into our life entered Gordon the social worker. Steven has always had a thing about lookalikes. He likes to match people from his everyday life with people off the telly. Steven thought that Gordon resembled Pete Hooton, the lead singer of The Farm which was uncanny as they were both from Liverpool. Steven and Gordon clicked very quickly. Gordon had a catchphrase: 'Good man' and Steven would greet him with a thumbs up and a 'Good man'. I suspect Gordon collided with his managers several times over Steven's case. He arranged a direct payments package which gave us a support worker for eight hours per week. There was a bit of money left over and as Steven had started to put on some medication-induced weight gain, I asked Gordon whether we could use the spare money to fund a personal trainer. His reply was that he thought it was 'a sound idea' but having since met his senior managers, I couldn't imagine them approving of the move. I'll be forever grateful for the time he really stuck his neck out for us: he'd just been to a multi-disciplinary meeting with a particularly hostile psychologist and a paediatrician. He was so appalled by their dismissive attitude towards Steven that he came round to give us 'a heads up'. That's what 'working with families' is all about in my book. Gordon was only around for 18 months, but years later another new social worker for Steven told us that Gordan had been his mentor when he first qualified, and described the impact Steven had on him. That feeling was entirely mutual.

Now we come to the tricky bit. Time to throw a few tomatoes. Steven was 16 and we were visited one day by his new social work 'transition manager'. I'm no psychic by any means, but I remember saying to Julie after that very first meeting that we needed to keep our third eye open with this one. The court prohibits me from naming her so we'll use Steven's long-established lookalike term of reference – 'Whistler's Mother'! If egos can be the sizes of countries, this woman was the Soviet Union. At the time we first met, one of Steven's classmates was in the Assessment and Treatment Unit (ATU) that Steven was to be detained in two years later. Whistler's Mother, even then, was pushing for Steven to spend some time in the unit but what struck me was that she kept describing Steven's mate's story as 'one of my biggest success stories', which was at complete odds to the stories I'd been hearing from the school staff about the lad's trauma caused by the detention. I've written loads about Whistler's Mother over the years, so I'll just add one final story. Whilst Steven was detained, I had a dream one night. The dream clarified a lot for my muddled thinking at the time and helped me with my sheer incapability of knowing how to handle WM. In the dream, I'm in a small motorboat on the Thames at Windsor. Coming towards me is a huge, pink inflatable bouncy castle that is occupying most of the river. Whistler's Mother is sitting on a throne on the inflatable, waving to the tourists in much the same way the real Queen might perform a few hundred yards from this dream setting. It is impossible not to collide with the inflatable. I'm sure you don't need your inner Carl Jung to spend too much time understanding that imagery. Suffice to say, it was daunting but a relief at the same time to realise that collision was inevitable, as it eventually was, although I didn't expect the collision to happen in the Royal Courts of Justice. Since the day in court, I've only seen Whistler's Mother once but she can still cast a long shadow over my psyche.

Thankfully, we got a new social worker for Steven – Collette. I don't envy Collette's position back then taking over. We'd been on the front pages of most of the main newspapers and social services had rightly come in for a lot of stick. She could have been daunted into becoming a bag of nerves, but she had a quiet confidence and a humanity that pierced straight through the defences I'd erected after four years of Whistler's Mother. Collette bonded very quickly with Steven over a mutual interest in The Pet Shop Boys. She understood Steven's boundaries so never imposed herself after their introductory chat about Neil Tennant's hat collection. There's a lot of rubbish written about 'best interests' when it's clearly someone else's best interests that are in play, but I always felt that Collette had Steven's best interests at the forefront of everything she did. She helped me get shot of the overbearing learning disabilities psychologist. She stood up to the positive behaviour team when she could see we were drowning in functional analysis logs. And she played a blinder in getting Steven his first home of his own after we were made homeless. After three years, she was moved on to another post and we've had a succession of social workers since. But each time a new one arrives they always say, 'Collette sends her regards'. That's such a tiny thing, but it means a lot. A human contact. Writing this Foreword, I'm struck by how each of these five social workers in our lives has reappeared just when we thought the relationship was over. I think there's a message in there. For me, the social work described in this book is about building relationships. Human, trusting relationships. And any relationship worth its salt is going to have a lifelong impact. The five social workers I've written about played a part in some of the most difficult, or powerful times in my life and their influence, good or bad, will be with me forever.

Mark Neary, father to Steven and author

Acknowledgements

To Karen and David Maude for very carefully reading earlier drafts of the chapters and making considered responses to them, including a forensic eye to use of punctuation. To Nina Riddlesden, Shvonne Nakonecznyi, Jack Skinner, Ryan Cowley and Fazeela Hafejee for sharing your stories and for responding to the 'You the social worker' scenarios at the end of each chapter.

To Professor Chris Hatton for contesting and/or supporting ideas explored in this book and for encouraging us to commit our thoughts to paper. To Paul Richards and the Stay Up Late campaign for showing us there is a better way and that there is no tablet too big that it can stop a good night out. To Lead the Way, Bradford Talking Media and others who have welcomed us into their lives and kept us focused on us why social work matters.

We want to express our particular thanks to others who have inspired us including bloggers Sara Ryan, Mark Neary and Mark Brown; your blogs are joyous, beautiful, witty, heartbreaking, frustrating and anger inducing in the most unexpected measures. The stories you have chosen to share about your lives and the experiences of your families and loved ones has had a huge impact on our thinking and feelings about social work.

Most importantly we want to thank the people we serve, the people who allow us into their lives and share their innermost thoughts with us. They tell us their aspirations and passions, their goals and desires as well as their frustrations and anger, with us, with the world.

It is a privilege to be invited as a guest into your lives.

Preface

*People with disabilities, both mental and physical, have the
same human rights as the rest of the human race... This flows
inexorably from the universal character of human rights, founded
on the inherent dignity of all human beings. (paragraph 45)*

Brenda Hale, Baroness Hale of Richmond [2014] UKSC 19 on
appeal from: [2011] EWCA Civ 1257; [2011] EWCA Civ 190

It was 3a.m., and we were still all in the bar. The guy serving us
drinks had listened to us talking about this idea we had for a book.
He nodded and asked, 'What's your book about?'

After taking a minute to think, one of us replied, 'It's 3a.m. It's
way past our bedtimes. But here we are talking to you because we
are adults and we are free to choose to be here, doing this. The only
people who should have bedtimes are children and people who've
been imprisoned for serious crimes.'

That's what our book's about. This book tells stories of just how
powerful social work can be. At its heart are stories drawn from
frontline practice.

The idea for the book had its roots in open access online
blogs which the authors started to write in 2015. They served as
a way of reflecting on and thinking about what we were reading
and hearing about social work. We are Elaine James, Researcher and
Commissioner in Public Health and Disability; Rob Mitchell,
Principal Social Worker; Hannah Morgan, Senior Lecturer in
Disability Studies and Director of the Centre for Disability Research
at Lancaster University; Mark Harvey, Principal Social Worker; and
Ian Burgess, Social Worker and Mental Capacity Lead. We didn't
know if anyone else would be interested, whether our thoughts

would resonate and connect with others. However, in just three years the blog had been read over 35,000 times by people living in 91 countries around the world. As interest in the blog grew, our confidence also grew that we were saying something about social work which others recognised and wanted to read about.

The stories we have chosen for this, our first, book are curated and edited from those original reflective blogs. The blogs are still available to read in their original forms on the blog sites. Taken together they form an extended and updated collection where we revisit and explore the issues in more detail. We hope to encourage others to experiment with social work, be creative and test the edges of their own practice.

We also hope that in reading this collection, you will have an appreciation of how important the social model of disability is to social work. We believe that social work is human rights in practice, and that the role of social workers is to uphold the inherent dignity of those people whose lives they are privileged to be a part of.

As co-authors, we came together through work connections formed on the social media platform, Twitter. Our Twitter handles are @ElaineLJames, @RobMitch92, @HannahnagroM and @Mwharvey.

However, we bonded over a shared love of the creative arts including music, writing, cinema and photography. Three of us are social workers; two are researcher practitioners working in commissioning and social work education. We share a commitment to practitioner and scholar activism that seeks to influence debates about our profession and that lead to better outcomes for people who use adult social care. We resist 'them' and 'us' dichotomies; all of us have experience of social workers who have been involved in the lives of our family members. We hope that by sharing our own experiences we will encourage others to join the debate and share their stories about social work.

We are optimistic for the future of the profession and we hope that our original blogs, and the updated versions published in this book, reflect our optimism.

We hope this book will provide learning and opportunities for reflection – whether you are a social work student who will find yourself graduating and applying for your professional practice role this year, or an experienced practitioner who believes that you should never stop learning and be open to critical reflection on your practice.

This is truly the best job in the world. You have the chance to inspire, challenge, provoke, reflect and make a real difference to people's lives. Never feel embarrassed talking about love and hope. Expect to make mistakes, it's only human; be open and honest when you do, and you will find they make you a better social worker. Never compromise on upholding rights and being an advocate for social justice. Prepare yourself. Take a deep breath. Step into the messy stuff with us!

About the authors

Elaine James has worked in various grant making and commissioning roles across children and adult social care for over 20 years. She is an honorary researcher at Lancaster University.

Rob Mitchell is a Principal Social Worker; he co-chaired the national Principal Social Worker Network for two years, is a Trustee of the National Social Work Awards and he is an Honorary Senior Lecturer at Lancaster University.

Dr Hannah Morgan is a Senior Lecturer in Disability Studies, Department of Sociology, Lancaster University and Director of the Centre for Disability Research (CeDR).

Mark Harvey is a Director of Disability Services in a Local Authority; he also co-chaired the national Principal Social Worker Network.

Ian Burgess is a social worker, Best Interest Assessor and Mental Capacity Lead.

Introduction

Welcome to the Messy Stuff

ELAINE JAMES, ROB MITCHELL and HANNAH MORGAN

Making the case for rights-based social work

We are proud to be associated with social work, a profession which is both intellectual and vocational in nature. We recognise the privileged access social work has to the intimacy of people's wishes, hopes, fears and personal beliefs.

Social workers hold a unique position in being both the advocate for the person to live their life in a manner which others may deem unwise, and yet also being the safeguard when someone is deprived of their liberty to protect them and others from risk.

For us, social work is a profession which positively embraces ambiguity and all the associated emotional complexity which other professions avoid. Social workers are agents of social justice, charged with upholding values of human dignity, equality, democracy and freedom. We make no apologies that we do not believe social work to be neutral or to operate in a neutral environment and as such our construction of social work throughout this book adopts a principled and passionate position on a range of issues.

However, we hope that for the reader this makes for a more interesting provocation. You might not always agree with the authors of this book, but the issues we raise are at the heart of current social work practice in adult social care – what matters is that we all engage in these debates, question our own assumptions and be the professional challenge to each other that we seek to be in our practice.

Since the 1970s successive UK policy makers have proposed a role for social workers in meeting the wider needs and aspirations of citizens by acting as a source of advice and connecting people into wider circles of support to sustain their independence and wellbeing. However laudable as a direction for social work this ambition may be, we argue it will fail to meet people's hopes, wishes and needs if social workers do not first have a strong understanding of the social model of disability, independent living and the forces of institutionalised disablism which they will need to overcome.

It is almost 40 years since Mike Oliver developed the social model of disability as a way of explaining the new approach to disability produced by the Union of the Physically Impaired Against Segregation (UPIAS) (Oliver 1990). However, social work still has a mixed relationship with the model, which challenges professionals as to whether they are prepared to give up professional power and devolve it back to people, recognising that people and communities hold the key to their own agency (Morgan and Roulstone 2012). As Oliver noted in *The Politics of Disablement*, 'in advancing the idea of independence, professionals and disabled people have not been talking about the same thing' (1990, p.91). While Oliver acknowledged that there had been attempts (by the late 1980s) to address this, his firm conclusion, and one that continues to resonate in 2019, was that 'power and control continue to remain with professional staff' which traps disabled people and professionals in dependency-creating relationships (1990, p.90).

Through our exploration of our personal histories and the retelling of stories and insights from our own practice we aim to make the case for values-driven, rights-based practice (Ife 2008). We hope this may offer a solution towards rebalancing the power in the relationship between people and the states they are citizens of in the manner envisaged in the *Disabled Adults and Social Workers Position Statement* and *Charter* published by the British Association of Social Workers (BASW) and Shaping Our Lives in 2016 (2016a, 2016b).

In 2018, the then Chief Executive of BASW, Ruth Allen, gave the following description of the profession:

Social work is about life, treasuring humanity, building connections, sharing and promoting fairness. It is about creativity, care and love

– being there to help people overcome obstacles and oppression that hold them back. For people using our services, a social worker should be someone to trust and believe in – someone who helps you believe in yourself. Sometimes we must hold boundaries, protect rights, advocate and challenge. We are always in the midst of the messy stuff, finding ways forward. (Allen 2018, p.27)

We are sometimes hurt by criticism of social work practice which comes from both within and outside of the profession. This is particularly the case where criticism is of individual social workers, and our alliance to the profession can take precedence over openness and reflexivity. However, we believe that it is only through a continued commitment to critical reflection, even when it is uncomfortable, that the profession will be able to properly listen and make the continual changes which keep our profession ethically grounded and relevant.

The authors have been privileged to have been invited into the lives of campaigning and voluntary organisations, led by self-advocates, including Shaping our Lives, Lead the Way, Bradford Talking Media and Stay Up Late. These organisations have told us that disabled people and others who use adult social care experience barriers which often relate to people's assumptions about their capacity and capabilities. They believe a social worker can support them and their peers to overcome these barriers by upholding their rights and enabling them to take positive risks in how they live their lives.

This work with such organisations resonates with the BASW and Shaping our Lives co-produced commitment (BASW 2016a, 2016b) to disabled adults and social workers working as equal partners through taking action together to:

- tackle physical, social, economic and other barriers to independent living, so that all disabled adults have the same choice, control and freedom as any other citizen – at home, at work, and as members of the community

- help disabled adults and social workers work better together to achieve the outcomes people want.

The most painful criticisms that we hear about social work come from those who have experienced the profession in the most traumatic and tragic circumstances.

These can come from parents whose children have experienced abuse and trauma whilst within services we have brokered and commissioned in the belief that it was in their best interest. This rocks our confidence in social work to the core.

If you are not yet aware of Sara Ryan, whose son Connor drowned in an NHS bath from neglect, then hopefully you will be inspired by reading this book to want to go and find out more and read about Connor's life.

We have been profoundly affected by our friendship with Mark Neary, a dad whose son Steven was unlawfully detained and deprived of his liberty in a residential care unit where workers abused and taunted him. Steven experienced terrible abuse, the trauma from which stayed with him, yet perhaps the most shocking aspect of his story is the small-minded nature of his treatment. Elaine James still remembers the tears which she couldn't control the first time she heard Mark talk about how the so-called care workers who were 'supporting' Steven invented a game where they would throw his socks into the garden when it rained to enjoy the spectacle of him falling in the mud, crying out as he ran out to retrieve them.

The profession must to be open to listening, critically reflecting and integrating the views of those who have experienced it at the worst of times if it is to continue to claim it has a legitimate role as an advocate for social justice.

The criticism of the social work Connor and Steven experienced is unfortunately not isolated. The following are illustrative of how significant the potential role is for social work to safeguard people's rights, delaying and preventing the need for services which may place them at enhanced risk of abuse and harm:

- 'An unduly casual attitude towards sudden death [and] inadequate systems for reporting incidents.' Ely Hospital Inquiry, 1969 (Socialist Health Association 2012).

- 'For long periods of time the hospital buildings were neglected and dangerous. Patients were sometimes soaked as they slept... Faeces and urine were frequently left unattended for days on end.' Normansfield Inquiry, 1978 (British Medical Association 1978).

- 'One person spent 16 hours a day tied to their bed or wheelchair, for what staff wrongly believed was for that person's own protection. One man told investigators that he had never chosen any of the places he had lived as an adult.' Cornwall, 2006 (Commission for Healthcare Audit and Inspection 2006).

- 'There were examples of individual patients in Winterbourne View Hospital and their families being threatened with the improper use of mental health legislation.' Winterbourne View Serious Case Review, 2012 (Flynn 2012).

- 'Residents would be taken there forcibly and left for hours, even overnight. They would not be let out until they had demonstrated their compliance by performing a care task; this could include being forced to clean up their own excrement.' Veilstone, 2017 (Day 2017).

- 'Staff threw cake which had been made by a resident at Hal's head when he requested a biscuit, he was given an onion to eat and when he would not eat it he was sent to his room; Hal paid for staff meals during outings.' Mendip House, 2018 (Flynn 2018).

Rather than being lost in the horror of Connor and Steven's experiences, we are drawn to the love we hear when their parents speak about them. The unconditional love that we hear when Sara and Mark talk about Connor and Steven is the key to good social work.

Good social workers practice with unconditional positive regard for the person they are supporting. This aspect of social work practice unites in common cause those who are newly entering the profession with those whose experience holds together established teams.

A new start for social work with adults

We believe we are at the dawning of a new start for social work with adults, one that we hope will see the days of social workers being reduced to managers and brokers of care disappear into the history book of things we did and then realised were not a great idea.

Care management shackled the profession; we see the shackles being rejected and discarded by emboldened social workers who are reclaiming their professional identity. Creative approaches towards reclaiming and reimagining the social work role have been particularly embraced by adult social workers who are attempting to define their unique role relative to the people they serve within the added complexity of their practice being integrated into health and social care teams. We felt the sea change in adult social work with the Mental Capacity Act 2005.

For the first time since the implementation of the NHS and Community Care Act 1990 it was possible to see a uniquely defined role emerge for social workers that required the profession to properly advocate for people and to work to promote the inherent principles and values which make social work practice better.

Adult social work in England has for a long time suffered for being a so-called 'Cinderella service', poorly resourced when compared with social work in children's services and facing systematic attempts to deskill the professional role into that of unqualified care manager (Dominelli 2009). For social workers like us, who felt a passion for working with adults and found ourselves lost amongst the rise of the care managers, swimming around looking for something to cling on to that we recognised as real social work, the Mental Capacity Act 2005 was vital in rediscovering ourselves. The creation of Best Interest Assessor (BIA) roles – the unique role that social workers now take of safeguarding people's inherent dignity, ensuring their wishes are central to any decision taken in their best interest and in promoting the notion that human rights are universal – gives us lots of confidence for the future.

The world turned further when the English social work employers' organisation, the Association of Directors of Adult Social Services, published jointly with Skills for Care a guidance note (ADASS 2012) arguing that rather than being merely brokers and managers of care, social work as a profession 'is underpinned by core values and behaviours that work with and empower individuals, families and communities' (p.1) within the boundaries of the international definition of social work.

We were further emboldened when, in 2012, the then College of Social Work published *The Business Case for Social Work with Adults*

(TCSW 2012), which called for social workers to be 'freed from the shackles of care management' (p.3) so that they could focus properly on promoting active citizenship, a role which it was argued social work was uniquely prepared to undertake because social work education fosters the social capital that makes active citizenship in thriving communities a genuine possibility.

Our confidence blossomed when two years later in 2014, the International Association of Schools of Social Work General Assembly, the International Federation of Social Workers and the British Association of Social Workers adopted a new global definition for social work which firmly placed human rights at the heart of the definition of the role:

> Social work is a practice-based profession and an academic discipline that promotes social change and development, social cohesion, and the empowerment and liberation of people. Principles of social justice, human rights, collective responsibility and respect for diversities are central to social work. Underpinned by theories of social work, social sciences, humanities and indigenous knowledge, social work engages people and structures to address life challenges and enhance wellbeing. (IFSW 2014)

The arguments continue, however, as to how well individual social workers on the front line are supported and encouraged to integrate their own humanity into their practice (Werkmeister Rozas and Garran 2016) and uphold the rights of others to be seen as fully human with equal access to the full range of human rights (James, Harvey and Mitchell 2017). We hope that this book will make a positive contribution to this debate, arguing the case for a reimagined social work role, as both applied social scientist and creative artist, steeped in the social model of disability and as an expert in equality, mental capacity and human rights law (Croisdale-Appleby 2014).

Erroneous associations between the concepts of risk and danger have become normative as reasons for referral for social workers to be asked to intervene in people's lives. However, we believe social workers taking a rights-based approach, which recognises the person as the expert of their life and circumstances, offers an alternative perspective to the big questions facing health and social care over the next 20 years – those of meeting the needs of an ageing population and of children and young people living with multiple health care needs.

As authors, we share a positive belief in people and a passionate commitment to uphold people's right to self-determination. People are the experts of their own lives; their wishes, feelings and beliefs should direct how they are supported to live them.

The act of writing the blogs from which this book developed served as a form of creative expression which we took pleasure from, and we hope that readers might consider the potential rewards and value they may get from actively engaging in similar reflective exercises. We hope you enjoy reading this book as much as we enjoyed writing it!

What this book will cover

Our approach to social work is grounded in the idea of being servants, not masters, of people whose lives social workers have the privilege to be a part of.

We argue that rights-based social work practice requires critical thinking about the role of the social worker as an agent of social justice. We believe that social work interventions are not neutral and that the very act of attempting to understand any complex human system will result in attempts being made to change it. We describe a role for social work as an active agent, tackling the structural causes of disadvantage and injustice, with social workers assuming the role of accomplice in subverting the status quo enough to disrupt and effect positive and sustainable change. We begin to introduce the idea that the nature of social work is transitional, with social workers being agents of adaptation and change. Finally, we reflect on the expectation that social workers are there at points in time when there is the potential for social change and problem solving in human relationships and encourage self-reflection on our role in people's lives.

In Chapter 2 we argue that integrating human rights within social work practice is entirely consistent with the global definition of social work and the profession's mission to promote social justice. We suggest that rights-based practice requires social workers to embrace socio-legal practice which amplifies people's voices and ensures their wishes, feelings and beliefs are central to decision making.

We further expand on this argument in Chapter 3, where we present our view that a person's sense of wellbeing is entangled with their sense of being accepted and belonging to their community. We argue that social work transcends being merely an agent of the state but rather is a global profession with a global identity. Social workers have a role in securing justice for those who are denied the right to a relationship, the right to marry and have children, the right to register to vote and participate in elections, and the right to have a job and own a house.

In Chapter 4 we reflect on how, as our health and social care systems remain stubbornly fixed on old-style models of investing in ill health, there will be a continuing role for social workers in advocating for people's right to be recognised as active citizens whose agency is central to living happy, healthy lives. We consider using human rights as a reflective tool to encourage social workers to challenge themselves and the often taken-for-granted assumptions that their involvement in people's lives is helpful.

In Chapter 5 we expand this further, presenting critically reflective, rights-based social work practice with adults as being more than a simplistic repositioning of ideas of risk management, rights and responsibilities. We describe our critically reflective social worker as one who works in partnership with people to co-create the future they want. We note how adult social work is increasingly being tested within public arenas such as the media and the courts. Public scrutiny is rightly challenging the approach social workers have taken to answer the moral and ethical dilemmas they face when balancing their professional judgement between protection imperatives and the desire to uphold personal autonomy. We argue that each case ruling before the Courts brings a further refinement of thinking about the nuances within human rights law, including the Mental Health Act 1983 and the Mental Capacity Act 2005, with significant implications for the profession.

In Chapter 6 we argue that good social work practitioners use critically reflective supervision to incorporate theory, academic literature and continuing professional development to inform and explore wider practice and societal issues, seeking to find alternatives that promote choice, rights, autonomy, partnership and control.

And finally, in our closing chapter we conclude that in order to keep social work relevant we need to reclaim the profession by paying attention to creative approaches which innovate and improve our relationships with the people we are here to serve. We advocate for a new bohemian movement in social work which blends the positive, progressive and creative with a humanist understanding of the art of people, cultures, love and a dash of science to add colour.

Chapter 1

Servants Not Masters

ELAINE JAMES, ROB MITCHELL and HANNAH MORGAN

Introduction

In this chapter we introduce you to our approach towards social work, which is rights-based (Ife 2008) and draws on a strong tradition of critically reflective practice introduced in the seminal text by Donald Schön, *The Reflective Practitioner* (1983).

Schön defined reflective practice as being the way that professionals become aware of their implicit knowledge base and learn from their experience through both reflection in action as it happens and reflecting on action after the event. Throughout this book we hope to set out how we have gone about thinking and learning through actions which have enabled us to test, critique and expand the substance of our knowledge about social work. Our construction of social work recognises that it does not operate in a neutral environment and the decisions that social workers take, and their reflection in and on practice, are partisan acts. We propose social workers as agents of social justice, upholding values of dignity, equality, democracy and freedom, which inevitably drive social workers towards making attempts to change the complex and messy lives of the people they support. Reflection both in and on action helps practitioners resist this urge, this protection imperative, which compels them towards imposing a new world order on the person. Holding true – to ensure that the outcome from all and every social work assessment is necessary, proportionate and upholds the wishes, feelings and beliefs of the person – is our social work mission. In 2011, Lord Justice Munby, at a speech given to social workers, asked the question – at what price did social workers 'safeguard' people by restricting their freedoms? His observation, that the local authority is a servant, not a master, is a touchstone for our practice, reminding us that we are there to uphold the inherent dignity of the people whose lives we become a part of. We are not there to displace their autonomy and impose a set of outcomes which we feel good about, but which steamroll their views and ignore their rights.

> The Local Authority is a servant, not a master…vulnerable adults… do not seek to be 'controlled' by the State… 'working together' involves something more, much more, than merely requiring carers to agree with a local authority's decision even if, let alone because, it is backed by professional opinion. (Munby 2011)

Is social work rocket science?

ROB MITCHELL

Is social work complex, like rocket science? I am still not sure. I've heard social work described as being harder than rocket science (which I suppose isn't hard if you are an actual rocket scientist) and I've heard it described as being simple common sense (which I am always sceptical about). I think I have come to the conclusion that social work practice isn't really complex but as the Chief Executive of the British Association of Social Workers said in 2018, it is working with complexity (Allen 2018). Social work is deep in the messy stuff, the grey areas of life, which is then fused with binary legislation and mixed with the social worker's interpretation of what we think we see in the smallest snapshot glimpse of someone's life. And like all our lives it's murky, confused, confusing, laced with double standards and things that you just can't properly explain to anyone.

Despite the million and one different variables in people's lives that social workers find, I do think as social workers we can identify much of what we hear and see in terms of four outcomes. Referencing Neil Kirk, the Prime Minister of New Zealand in the early 1970s, who is attributed with having said 'all most people want is somewhere to live, somewhere to work, someone to love and something to hope for' (Keane 2015), I would suggest social work is about: Love, Work, Home and Hope.

People don't tend to want more than these four things. Complexity might attract the 'professional' (those who are also drawn to blue lights, rushing into the Big Cases ready to be the Decision Maker), however the genuine complexity (i.e. the messy stuff which isn't easily solved with a set of pink papers or a court order) is usually left to someone else to sort as the blue light professional moves on to their next case, never looking back to check on how the person's life continues.

In my experience, of the four outcomes, Hope is first among equals. Hope is about ambition, a belief in a better future, not only for us but for our families and for others. Hope should be about ambitions without ever been dismissed as over ambitious. For social workers, I feel that working with people to enhance hope and opportunity, means that we need to be able to critically evaluate everything, and mostly ourselves and our own worth, to the person and their family and friends. Do we enhance the outcomes that people want? Do we enable relationships to thrive regardless of the difficulties they may cause us (anyone wish to displace this troublesome Nearest Relative?). Do we take a risk-enabling approach to enhance relationships and help provide loving relationships to replace us? Do we genuinely strive to support people to achieve social status? To evaluate everything means to evaluate ourselves.

We are at our best when we believe in people. We are the only profession that is taught to do that. We believe that people are good and where they are not, we work to alter factors around them to facilitate change and ensure good. To believe in people is to believe in Hope. If the outcome is a nursing home, what is our approach to Hope and ambition within that? If people want to scale an active volcano, or become prime minister, or race high speed cars, is it not our job to hear their voices and positively engage with their wishes, feelings and beliefs to help them construct the world they want for themselves? One in which they can experience happiness?

Maybe it's time for us to slightly reframe ourselves as social workers. I have felt I have peddled a worn-out bag of care management tricks for years and generally the tricks don't work. The very things we do to keep people 'safe' are the very things that expose them to classical health risks for dull, restricted and inactive lifestyles. Our illusion and box of tricks are seen through (just ask people with learning disabilities and their families); the tricks may be disappearing, but we remain – social workers laid bare without the tricks and care plans (including the less than visible 'fairer' charges'). Social work is reclaiming its purpose, upholding social justice by advocating for values of inherent dignity, equality, democracy and freedom.

So, are we ready to let go of the box of tricks? Are we ready to stand beside people and their families now without claiming we have a bag of magic tricks? Can we talk honestly about the illusion they are and instead be clear there are no complex shortcuts to life and no day care or home care or care home that's likely to mend the broken heart or fulfil potential or lead to a world of things that we might have? And if there are four things that people want and need, Love, Work, Home, Hope, what's our role? These things are messy and will involve us exercising humility. We are not the professional expert. People and their families are the experts of their own lives that we really know so very little about. Our unique professional role may be keeping the hope alive.

Aligning values and nurturing resilience

In the UK, the traditional route of employment for social workers is within local authorities; these are administrative structures which provide functions laid out in statute and codified in UK law. Social workers providing statutory functions on behalf of local authorities are also found working for NHS health providers. Social workers practising the core skill sets they learned during their degree also work within voluntary sector organisations, community groups and in social enterprises. Increasingly, social work employers also secure social work services through employment agencies on a short-term, temporary basis. For social workers with a strong ethical drive for their chosen profession, the extent to which an employer offers moral management, through a culture which makes explicit an ethical commitment in the moral contact between social worker and social work employee, is particularly important. Lawler and Bilson (2010) argue that social workers are more likely to respond to, connect with and follow leadership from their employer where there is a strong alignment with their values base. Edgar Schein (2004), in his classic study of organisational culture and its impact on employee commitment, proposed that most people form a strong self-concept to protect their core values, developing what he termed a 'career anchor' which they rely on to hold their internal values base together during the changes they experience in their career. Career anchors function as a stabilising force and can be thought of as the values and motives that the person will not give up if forced to make a choice. Finding a social work employer whose culture is to nurture and sustain relationships whilst supporting people to develop at their own pace is worth the research time, as it is more likely such an employer is congruent with your social work values and is a place where you can be happy in work.

With the rapidly changing policy context surrounding social work and the advent of new technologies redefining the very nature of work in public service, the range of employment options available are increasingly diverse. Some find turbulence and change stimulating; a creative environment where they can thrive. Others find it dizzying, seeking instead stability and clarity in terms of their employers' expectations of them. All these experiences are also shared by the people social workers serve, an insight which good social workers will recognise. Wherever you choose to practice, the ethical challenge faced by every social worker is aligning your values with that of your employer and the resilience challenge is becoming skilled in handling ambiguity and change. Social work can be emotionally challenging. It is even harder if you are faced with managing the compromise between your social work values and those of your employer. Forming supportive peer networks, with other social workers whose intrinsic motivation and values reflect your own, matters. However, resilience needs to be nurtured; good employers care about and provide manageable caseloads, access to resources, quality reflective supervision and continuing professional development pathways. Psychologist Frederick Herzberg, in his two factor theory of intrinsic employee motivation (1959), argues that to be 'happy' in work, employees need more than traditional objective rewards of progression through the hierarchy and enhanced packages of remuneration, but rather they need to experience achievement through personal recognition, being assigned and able to create and invest their energy in interesting and intellectually stimulating work, being trusted to assume increased levels of responsibility and being able to progress in their careers supported through opportunities for learning which align to their values base. Women as social workers face further barriers to accessing Herzberg's motivational factors. Mainiero (1994) argues that for women to be successful in complex working environments, such as those experienced by social workers, adapting and surviving the competition for resources and advancement, they need to develop advanced political skills which enable them to outcompete their male colleagues. Mainiero proposes what she calls her four stages of maturation by which female managers acquire these political skills, starting from a position of political naïveté as they enter the workplace, through building credibility and refining a style over time in readiness for ultimately shouldering responsibility.

Our experience is that social workers who embrace the concept of being continuous learners, investing in their own professional development and encouraging others to do the same, are the most confident and happiest in work and most committed to advancing the social work mission. Continuing professional development encourages active links to be made between theoretical frameworks and social work practice which support critical reflection and thinking about what worked and why. Investment in higher-level, post-qualifying social work education also supports a continuous cycle of adaptive learning, discovery and invention which enables you to keep your practice relevant and resolve any potential conflicts between what you are experiencing and your social work values.

Conflict between experience in practice and values is a continued source of tension for social workers. Social work's mission, as described in the British Association of Social Workers' code of ethical practice, is to uphold respect for the inherent dignity, equality and worth of all people in keeping with the United Nations Declaration of Human Rights (1948), through upholding social justice both in relation to the individual they are supporting and wider society. The contentious point for social workers who want to advocate a rights-based approach is that you can only be a servant not a master if your employer supports you to be able to practise in a way which enables you to spend time with people, taking all practicable steps to find out what they want from you and why. Working for a social work employer with a relational and rights-based ethos makes it much easier to live the values of an ethical practitioner than being in a highly rigid care management environment where your core function is to broker care packages and move the person on to the next setting as quickly as possible. Rights-based employers encourage what O'Donnell *et al.* (2008) termed a form of ethical activism. Ethical activism is a more radical approach to social work, with social workers positioned as being more than allies working within a network of support around people, but rather assuming the role of accomplice in subverting the status quo enough to disrupt and effect positive change. You will know if you are working for a rights-based employer if you find yourself in the middle of ethical deliberations with people, their families and/or carers and other professionals on a regular basis. Ethically activist social work employers have a culture where every day brings a new debate about the ethics of any given intervention or approach, always centred on upholding the rights of the person social workers are supporting. Ethically activist social workers strongly argue to uphold people's wishes and feelings and are ready to tackle the politics and power dynamics which are pushing for unnecessarily disproportionate restrictive interventions.

An example of this in practice is the ruling on the *Wye Valley NHS Trust v Mr B* (2015) case, which was about a 73-year-old gentleman with a long history of mental health needs and poorly controlled diabetes. Following the death of his partner, Mr B lived on his own. He developed a leg ulcer, which did not heal over time, leading to a hospital admission in 2014. During a long stay in hospital, Mr B resisted treatment for his diabetes and his ulcer, which led to his leg becoming seriously infected. In 2015, the NHS trust who were caring for Mr B applied to the Court of Protection asserting that Mr B needed to have his leg amputated to save his life but lacked the capacity to make the decision, so they wanted Court authorisation to proceed. The evidence presented to the court made it clear that Mr B was likely to die within days from the infection if no action was taken; however if his leg was amputated, he had a positive life expectancy in excess of three years. Most people just remember it as the Wye Valley case, forgetting Mr B, the appellant. However, Justice Peter Jackson did not make such a crude error. Entirely centred on Mr B, and his views, the ruling upheld that whilst Mr B lacked capacity, this did not negate his known wishes, feelings, beliefs and values. In paragraph 11 of the ruling Peter Jackson noted that:

> This is not an academic issue, but a necessary protection for the rights of people with disabilities. As the Act and the European Convention make clear, a conclusion that a person lacks decision-making capacity is not an 'off-switch' for his rights and freedoms. To state the obvious, the wishes and feelings, beliefs and values of people with a mental disability are as important to them as they are to anyone else and may even be more important. It would therefore be wrong in principle to apply any automatic discount to their point of view.

Given these considerations, the judge ruled that it was not in Mr B's best interests to undergo an enforced amputation and ruled against the NHS Trust. This is what makes the Wye Valley case ruling so important for social workers: this emphasis on the person's *wishes* and *feelings* when constructing a best interest decision. It is a simple message: the person's views are central.

The Wye Valley case reminds us that it is really important for social workers to have a good grasp on legislation and case law. Take as an example where you find yourself allocated to a case where the previous professional has misquoted the views of an advocate and missed the fact that the person clearly doesn't want to be in the care home they are living in. The first steps you should take as a rights-based social worker could be to arrange a visit and meet the person concerned and their advocate, to find out for yourself what their views were, essentially starting the process of building a relationship and working with the person on what their wishes and feelings are to inform the best interest recommendation. One of our social workers told us about such a case, where he was unpicking previous decision making that had separated Mavis (not her real name) and her husband of over 60 years, Johnny (also not his real name). Johnny was her advocate and was very clear that her wishes, when she had had capacity, were to go home. He wanted her to come home making a strong case that in 60 years they had never been apart. He did not understand why no one would listen to them. The social worker had spoken to Johnny before he met with the couple together at the care home. Johnny told the social worker how he visited Mavis every single day. He took her out to a local café a couple of days a week as they had always enjoyed a cup of tea and a scone. Johnny wanted to impress on the social worker that Mavis had been a tennis player – not just any tennis player; she had been the all-county champ. The minute he met Mavis, the social worker knew the assessment was not going to follow a traditional path. Mavis was polite but was not to be directed. As anticipated by her husband Johnny, she wanted to talk about tennis and her life as a tennis player. As he listened to her talk, the social worker pondered about his assessment, eventually reaching the conclusion, 'Tennis matters, I will make sure to write it down.'

The care home staff were surprised when the social worker asked them about her love of tennis. They were unable to tell the social worker anything about Mavis, including how she even came to be in care. They didn't know that she liked scones either. The social worker found himself thinking, 'How can you genuinely deliver person-centred care to Mavis if you don't know what she likes?' The question played on his mind as he drove back to the office.

With each passing visit, the social worker found himself thinking he could sit and listen to Mavis for hours. Eventually she moved on from talking about tennis, and finally began to speak about how devoted she was to her husband Johnny and how safe she felt when she was with him. The social worker got the strong impression that her husband and their life together was everything to her. Life without him wasn't worth living. Mavis didn't want to be at the care home, she just did not feel this was her home. She had a home; it was with Johnny. 'They do alright here but it's not for me. Not my cup of tea, love. I don't need to be here, Johnny will look after me', she said. The social worker wrote it all down. He made some enquiries and established that both Mavis and Johnny were not happy with the arrangements and had asked if it would be possible for her to go home with some home care support. The home was of the view that Mavis was not much bother, a good resident. But yes, they were aware that she never really came out of her room except when Johnny visited and yes, she did seem very quiet. The social worker said he would take this further and left.

The move for Mavis to a care home had been arranged by a nurse who was commissioning her nursing care. The social worker set up a meeting to talk through options to get Mavis home. At first things went well as the nurse and social worker agreed that Mavis lacked the capacity to understand, retain, weigh up and communicate some of the risks associated with her living at home. However, something changed when, despite this, the social worker proposed a plan to get Mavis home in keeping with her previously known wishes and feelings. The nurse stopped the social worker mid-sentence, saying, 'What do you mean the person is objecting? She doesn't have capacity.' Having avoided dropping his tea in surprise, the social worker patiently explained that in keeping with Mavis's wishes, it was their job as professionals to look at her going home before any other options were considered. Everyone has wishes or feelings, everyone, was the point the social worker made, and you must take those into account in all decisions. After discussing the situation in more depth with the nurse, it became clear that until recently, Mavis had been extremely unwell. The nurse was very worried that if Mavis returned home, her physical health would decline and she would become unwell again. The social worker found himself arguing that being well cared for includes emotional needs as well as physical. Mavis did not care about being physically well; she cared about being with her husband, even if this meant she shortened her life.

People with capacity have the right to autonomy over their own body; an adult who is not able to consent cannot be held against their will without consideration of their rights, wishes or the law. When a person lacks capacity, however, as with the Wye Valley case, it seems that there is the potential for these rights to be eroded, for other considerations to be applied which raise the bar against which people are tested. Article 5, the right to liberty, and Article 8, the right to a private and family life, of the European Convention on

Human Rights should trip off the tongue of everyone working across health and social care. Interpretation of Article 8 is really broad. Social workers risk being charged with interference with someone's Article 8 rights simply by being there. Social workers are guests in people's lives, interfering in their private and family space – which may be justified – but it cannot just be assumed that involvement is always good or benign.

After conversations with the nurse and various other members of the multi-disciplinary team, the social worker and nurses agreed to fund a joint package of care to get Mavis home. However, as the panel meeting ended agreeing the plan, the social worker heard an ominous warning from the commissioner that setting up the home care would not be quick. A few weeks later, a phone call came through from Johnny saying that he was at the end of his tether; nothing had changed, and he wanted the case to go to the Court of Protection to challenge the continued detention of Mavis against her wishes. The social worker's heart sank. He wanted what Johnny and Mavis wanted: for her to go home. It broke the social worker's heart that they weren't together. The social worker was left with the impression that for others involved in arranging the care and support for Mavis, her human rights were a distraction from their core business of keeping her physically healthy; her emotional wellbeing a secondary issue to her body mass index and Waterlow score for risk of developing pressure ulcers.

Blog writer Lucy Series observes that a small proportion of people who are objecting to being detained in a care home actually proceed before the court, and some die before their case is fully heard (Series 2019). In this case, however, the challenge was heard by the court, whereby the judge ordered that in keeping with Mavis's wishes, home care must be arranged to help Mavis to return to her home with Johnny. The plan was enacted, and a provider brokered within a week under pressure from the court. Unfortunately, it was too late. Whilst professionals argued, Mavis's heath had declined. Mavis died in her sleep that weekend, in the care home. Johnny was the eighth person to be informed of her passing.

Eldergill DJ commented in *Westminster City Council v Sykes* (2014):

> Risk cannot be avoided of course. All decisions that involve deprivation of liberty or compulsion involve balancing competing risks, of which the risk that others may suffer physical harm is but one. For example, detention and compulsory care or treatment may risk loss of employment, family contact, self-esteem and dignity; unnecessary or unjustified deprivation of liberty; institutionalisation; and the unwanted side-effects of treatment.
>
> [...]
>
> Therefore, it is her welfare in the context of her wishes, feelings, beliefs and values that is important. This is the principle of beneficence which asserts an obligation to help others further their important and legitimate interests. In this important sense, the judge no less than the local authority is her servant, not her master.

Transitions

Throughout a social work career, social workers will experience several transitional stages, each one marking changes both in terms of their professional status and their knowledge and understanding of what the role of the social worker is. William Bridges (2004) has written extensively about the potential impact these transitional phases can have. He helpfully describes a three-stage model for any transition, which starts with any new beginning first needing a process of ending to take place.

Endings can be quite an emotional time as they involve letting go of the things that matter to you. It can be quite a shock realising just how much you take for granted the personal networks that you form as you move on from being a student social worker into employment as an autonomous professional, move from one team to another, or move from one social work employer to another. There is a comfort that comes from the ritual and routines you build around yourself, and the familiarity of how the people in your network just know what you mean without you having to explain yourself. It can be quite a painful experience letting go of these stabilising and reinforcing structures in your life and entering a stage of liminality where you shed your old identity and prepare to become someone new (Morgan 2012; Turner 1969). To help you through this stage you might want to think about the following:

- Be open with others about what you are losing in making these changes in your life. Yes you are moving on to an exciting new phase, but things will not be the same.

- Treat with respect your friendships and professional networks; you never know when they may be useful in the future!

- Mark the ending and celebrate what really mattered about this stage of your life which you are now moving on from.

In Bridges' model, he describes a neutral zone which happens between the ending of the old and the beginning of the new. During this stage you may find yourself feeling a sense of disorientation as you realign from how things used to work to how things happen in the new world you have entered. This can be a very creative time when you can really experiment and potentially reinvent yourself and your practice. However, it can also be a stressful period when you can experience setbacks which relate to the losses you felt during the ending stage. To help you through this stage you might want to think about the following:

- Make the most of any training and continuing professional development you are offered, and which might help you make sense of how your new employers, colleagues and the people around you work.

- Resist any pressure to move on too quickly from the neutral zone; every transition is personal and should move at the pace which works for you.

- Be kind to yourself and only set yourself short-term goals. Don't try to plan for the long term yet!

Finally, when you are ready, Bridges proposes that you will transition into a new beginning which is the time for you to fully present your new identity, new energies and sense of purpose. During this time, be consistent in clearly describing to others what you are intending to do during this new stage of your life. Have a clear plan in mind which helps people understand how they can participate and be a part of your new world. If you invite people in and share the celebrations of each success with others, you will find people flock to you. Social work is a diverse profession – all voices are to be welcomed and encouraged. There are lots of ways that you can capture your personal social work journey and celebrate each of your successes. Creative expression is the hallmark of a good social worker; how you choose to do this should reflect who you are:

- Are you a poet, do you want to capture the images on camera or through film? Do you write or blog? You can be as creative as you want in telling your social work story.

- Keep connected to academic debate and research – try to read a social work journal once a fortnight to keep your thinking connected to the edge of practice and be open to other journals that can challenge and elevate your thinking such as those which publish research co-produced with people with experience in social work.

- You don't need anyone's permission – just go ahead and get on with creating new resources, materials, things to share with your colleagues. Once you start you will be amazed where creativity will take you.

What differs about the transitions social workers experience relative to other professional groups is the extent to which social work education emphasises critical reflexivity at the core of the ethical nature of the profession. The cyclical process of reflecting on experiences, learning and developing your insight and understanding of yourself as a professional will make you a better social worker. Use your reflective supervision as a time to check for warning signs of burn-out or its lesser known cousin, rust-out. Psychologists Leo Hendry and Marion Kloep (2002) argued that our development depends on our responses to challenges that we face during our lives and careers. How resilient you are is determined by what resources you can draw on when faced by the transitions at each stage of your career, the culture of your workplace, your social and professional networks and relationships, your own confidence and self-esteem, and your financial position. When these resources are low and you are faced with high demands you can find yourself facing burn-out. Social worker burn-out is well documented, with Eileen Munro in her 2011 review of child protection social work identifying a long list of issues which affect the wellbeing of individual social workers. But what about the risk of rust-out: reaching the point in your career where you have lots of resources surrounding you, but the job no longer excites and challenges you (Hendry and Kloep 2002)? Ask yourself at different stages of your career: Are you still making a positive difference or are you stagnating? Do you still have a strong sense of purpose and drive? Or are you in a dead-end and you can't see a way out? Are you still in the right place or is it time for a change? Is there a risk that you no longer feel a passion for social work, and, as a result, are you at risk of losing sight of the person, or people you are working with?

Conclusion

In this chapter we have introduced you to social work, which we believe is an amazing profession, and we welcome those who have joined it and chosen to be part of it and to engage with our view of what it can offer and how it can be. If, like us, you believe that social work is a vocation, a strong impulse or inclination to follow, a path rather than just a career, then you must also understand that the social worker is who you are, not what you are. You need to understand that when the job is not one of processing people into care but instead is true social work, it will be a continuous journey of critical reflection, new insights and learning. Through constantly adapting your social work approach during each transition you experience, reflecting on your own learning and applying that learning to how you approach and respond to the people whose lives you enter, you will become a better social worker.

Social work is about having an innate value base and a fire in your belly to live it and practise it. This has been squeezed out of some and become industrialised in others, with many a reason for that happening, but the key is releasing the phoenix from the fire.

There is not one type of social worker or one purest value base that makes social workers a single homogenous breed of either activists or state tools. There is, however, an expectation that social workers are there at points in time when there is the potential for social change, problem solving in human relationships and the empowerment and liberation of people to enhance their lives and freedoms. If in your career as a social worker you start to find that this stops for you at 5.30 p.m., then you need to have a good old social work self-reflection session and if it still stops for you at 5.30 p.m., then perhaps it never started at 9 a.m. in the first place.

Suggested further reading and resources

The suggested reading below is a helpful introduction if you want to read more about the ideas we discuss in this chapter:

British Association of Social Workers (2012) The Code of Ethics for Social Work. Accessed on 04/03/2019 at www.basw.co.uk/about-basw/code-ethics
Dominelli, L. (2009) *Introducing Social Work*. Cambridge: Polity Press.
Maclean, S., Finch, J. and Tedam, P. (2018) *Share: A New Model for Social Work*. Lichfield: Kirwin Maclean Associates Ltd.
Dr Lucy Series writes a blog on mental capacity and the law: https://thesmallplaces. wordpress.com/
Alex Ruck Keene also blogs extensively on Mental Capacity Case Law and Policy: www.mentalcapacitylawandpolicy.org.uk/

You are the social worker: Dan

Referral from Duty Team: 'Dan presented at reception this morning. He was very distressed and wanted to speak to a social worker, but he does understand he may have to wait until one is free to see him. He has had a row with his support workers as last night about some beer he had bought. He has hurt his foot, which on questioning he says was caused by him kicking the wall during the row.'

Dan is 18. He was taken into care when he was 4 and has an older sister who he was separated from whilst being moved between different residential care homes and foster care homes. He has recently moved out of a residential children's home as he is now 18 and too old to continue living there. He is currently living in a supported living flat with 24/7 staff. Dan has a support plan which states that he is supposed to have two-to-one support at all times.

When you visit Dan, he describes how frustrated he feels with the situation. He wants to live on his own in a flat in the block where his cousin lives. The support workers are very worried about this because they think his cousin is a bad influence on Dan and introduces him to drugs and alcohol. Dan says to you that the support workers are 'in his face' all the time. He explains that he hurt his foot kicking the wall during the argument with the support workers over him bringing a box of beer home, which he bought from the corner shop on the way home from a visit to his cousin. Dan didn't think that a few cans of beer were a big deal; he says he wasn't planning to drink on his own but to take them with him when he next visited his cousin. His foot really hurt when he woke up so after he had visited Duty to ask for a social worker to visit him, he had visited the hospital minor injuries unit and has had his foot checked out.

A social worker responds:

My experience of social work is that when a referral of this nature comes to our attention alarm bells immediately start ringing and as social workers, we heighten up levels of what we perceive to be risks to the individual. We start talking about safeguarding and in doing that we often provide additional services to mitigate risk, resulting in care provision being overly restrictive and unnecessary. It seems that this may have been the case for Dan given the suggestion in his support plan that he should have two staff with him all the time.

We must remember Lord Justice Munby and his challenge to us as social workers – what good is it making someone safer if it merely makes them miserable?

This case would be extremely worrying for me; not in orthodox terms of risk and safeguarding, but more in my view of poor social work interventions that Dan may have encountered since a very young age to result in such a restrictive placement at only 18. Immediately I would be beginning to think about Dan's human rights and how having this level of 'support' affects his human rights, in particular Article 8: the right to respect for private and family life, home and correspondence. Furthermore, I would investigate if the judicial authorisation of deprivation of liberty in settings outside hospitals and care homes had been undertaken in this situation as per the *Re X* (Court of Protection Practice) (2015) EWCA Civ 599 case, in relation to the increase in court applications for authorisation of deprivation of liberty safeguards following the Cheshire West decision in 2014.

The relationship between law and social work is of paramount importance and the legislation provides social workers with certain powers as well as duties that they are legally bound to fulfil. In this situation the following pieces of legislation will need to be considered:

- the Care Act 2014

- the Mental Capacity Act 2005

- the Human Rights Act 1998

- the Equality Act 2010

- the Children and Families Act 2014.

Dan, having reached the age of 18, is considered to be an adult. However, in any work I undertake with Dan, I would ensure that I took into consideration his early experiences, which could have had a long-term impact on his emotional and physical health, social development, education and future employment. The Care Act 2014 contains some important provisions relating to transition as teenagers approach adulthood. The concept of social identity is multi-dimensional and fluid to serve as a reminder that people are complex beings whose life experiences and backgrounds continuously impact on wellbeing and how they experience the world. A social worker should consider the Equality Act 2010 as a constituent part of the context in which we operate that underpins good, ethical practice through upholding values of equality and inherent dignity.

The scenario indicates that Dan has not been able to express his views to his support workers, or, if he has, then the support workers have failed to take his views into consideration. In this situation the approach I would undertake is less about risk management but more to develop a relationship with Dan in order to engage in a conversation and dialogue to find out what he wants to achieve/

outcomes and, from his perspective, how best to go about this. As Dan doesn't appear to have an appropriate adult (someone who isn't paid) to support him to make decisions he may be entitled to an independent advocate to ensure he can express his views and concerns. Any social work interventions with Dan should be looking at his strengths and assets. The focus would be on identifying and making the most of Dan's abilities and encouraging him to offer these skills and abilities as part of a positive contribution to achieve his outcomes. Encouraging opportunities to form new and engaging relationships will make people feel that they are making a positive contribution to their community and will in turn help them feel valued, not limited by their condition or circumstances. It feels that although Dan is currently attempting to seek support following a specific incident, there is a big piece of work to be undertaken in supporting him going forward to ensure that social work interventions are there to improve his life.

Everyone should have the opportunity to learn, form relationships and live their dreams and aspirations, while demonstrating how they can thrive and positively contribute to their local communities, not only achieving their own outcomes.

#LiveYourBestLife

Chapter 2

Mental Capacity, Mental Health and Least Restrictive Decision Making

ELAINE JAMES, IAN BURGESS, ROB MITCHELL and HANNAH MORGAN

Introduction

Human rights are enshrined in UK law dating back to the Magna Carta (1215), which established the principles of due process andequality:

> No free man shall be seized or imprisoned, or stripped of his rights or possessions, or outlawed or exiled, or deprived of his standing in any other way, nor will we proceed with force against him, or send others to do so, except by the lawful judgement of his equals or by the law of the land. (Clause 39 of Magna Carta)

The powers of English and Welsh law to detain people, including the Mental Health Act 1983 and Mental Capacity Act 2005, are rooted in these principles, that the state cannot act arbitrarily and detain a citizen on a whim.

The section that follows, 'Broken bones are easier to fix than a broken heart', was written by Ian Burgess, a social worker who has specialised in mental capacity law, in response to comments posted on social media platforms by commentators who observed that over ten years since the Mental Capacity Act 2005 (MCA) become law, most social work services were still talking about 'embedding the MCA'. That the Act had not been fully understood and implemented across health and social care was also one of the findings of the House of Lord's Select Committee's post-legislative scrutiny in 2014. To be still talking about some professionals not understanding the Act or not being aware of it cannot be acceptable. The Act encoded the natural rights of the individual to have their autonomy in decision making recognised into law in England and Wales. While these rights were still not being integrated into social work practice, the Act gave grounds for practice to be deemed to be unlawful. The blog is a reflection on how much easier people believe it is for health care professionals to diagnose and treat a physical health condition than for a social worker to work with the complexity of humanity. It made the case that if the statutory principles of the Act were applied correctly, with their instructions to social workers to be anti-discriminatory, to enable self-determination and to respect non-conformity, they would demystify what is unique about social work and provide for a defence to enable risk in decision making.

Broken bones are easier to fix than a broken heart

IAN BURGESS

Sometimes it is not that a professional is unaware of the human rights law which frames social work practice, but rather that they want to achieve a particular outcome, an outcome which they have themselves determined without the person being involved at all in the decision making. I have never challenged when I've found that a person lacks capacity to make a decision, only when I've concluded someone has capacity. The same occurs when a woman with dementia agrees with the professional who says she should go in a care home; she has capacity. But if she disagrees with the professional... You know the rest.

Apart from upholding a person's human rights and enabling autonomy, issues which trump any professional opinion about what is right or wrong for someone (otherwise people would never smoke cigarettes or drink alcohol!), there is also the small matter of professional respect. Last week I was standing next to a social worker, who was on the phone, listening to her trying to explain to a nurse how she had enabled a person with dementia to make the decision to return home. The social worker didn't say much and even from where I was standing, I could hear the nurse losing her temper until eventually the social worker looked up at me and said, 'She just hung up on me.'

Can you imagine a social worker approaching a nurse on a ward and criticising her skills at assessing wounds or inserting an intravenous cannula? Or how about a social worker telling an occupational therapist that his stairs assessment was wrong? Social workers are not trained or qualified to complete these tasks and would be wrong to not give the professional the respect they have earned. Even in the unlikely event they were present when those tasks or assessments were being completed, they would still not comment. And yet every week I hear from social workers who say that other professionals criticise their mental capacity assessments. Nearly always the other professional is not present so does not see what techniques the social worker applied in enabling the person to make the decision. It is not a bad idea to have others present so they can learn, but it is not always appropriate. But either way, it is shameful that one professional should feel able to openly criticise another, for example in a multi-disciplinary team meeting, about their professional conduct. And yet some do so without providing any evidence to show that they have also tried their best to enable the person to make the decision without success or without referring to what the law says about identifying the decision maker.

So why do some professionals want the person to lack the mental capacity to make the decision? I have sometimes sidestepped these disagreements about capacity and instead suggested we imagine for a moment the person doesn't have the capacity to decide. Then what? Because therein lies the reason. A capacity assessment which concludes the person cannot make the decision provides a means by which they can be forced into what is perceived by the professional to be a less risky situation, even though it is against the person's wishes and will make them unhappy. It is to use the law against the person.

Sometimes the professional says they have a duty of care towards the person, or it may be they are under pressure from family members or other colleagues for a particular outcome, or because a permanent move to a care home (for example) means a faster discharge from hospital or from a short stay placement. But more commonly it is because the professional doesn't want to get into trouble; it is easier to prove a person suffered broken bones than a broken heart.

None of those reasons are in the person's best interests. They are in the interests of other people.

Social workers have to be strong if they are to be able to hold true to their social work values. This requires practice leadership to provide the supportive framework which sustains innovation and practice leaders who can root and cultivate a culture based on trust at all levels. These are a prerequisite for social workers to question and challenge the status quo. Where social workers are led by legitimised practice leaders, who maintain the currency of their own professional education and provide a strong ethical basis for practice, they feel supported, safe and are positioned to hold risk and uphold the rights of the person. As a Mental Capacity Act Lead, I chair mental capacity clinics. At the clinics social workers can bring their mental capacity related queries, including their assessments for analysis, and are provided with written guidance. I also chair a more formal risk enablement panel. At the panel, the social worker gets management sign-off for a non-risk-averse decision to be made for an incapacitous person, one which respects the person's known wishes and feelings, is in the person's best interests and is the least restrictive option. The person is of course encouraged to attend; after all, 'no decision about me, without me' is the starting point. At the panel, we discuss collaboratively the consequences of one decision over another. Everyone is an equal in the discussion. Until 2007 social workers with adults lacked the legislative backing with which to challenge oppressive practice and promote independence. Championing human rights has become the raison d'être for social work.

> As observed by HHJ Cushing in the case of *P v Surrey County Council and Surrey Downs CCG* (2015) EWCOP 54 there are *positive obligations* incumbent upon social workers as agents of the state in the UK to ask themselves three critical questions when considering whether a care home is genuinely the least restrictive option:
>
> What harm, if any, may P suffer if his continued detention is authorised?...
>
> What placement or type of placement would be a more appropriate response?
>
> How long will it take to investigate the availability and suitability of a more proportionate response?

Best interest and least restrictive practice

The creation of the European Convention of Human Rights (ECHR) in the 1950s sought to ensure that all the states in Europe committed to respecting the fundamental rights of their citizens. The ECHR includes in Article 5 the right that no one shall be deprived of their liberty except in (certain) circumstances...and in accordance with a procedure prescribed by law. A circumstance which may engage Article 5 of the ECHR is that of 'unsound mind'. It is, therefore, legitimate for the state to detain a person on the basis of mental disorder – as long as there is a procedure and as long as there is an avenue of appeal to a court or tribunal.

Where people 'are not considered capable' (Percy Commission 1957, Section 169), further procedural safeguards exist within UK mental health law. Historically, the doctrine of parens patriae ('the parent of the Country') was the legal basis for surrogate decision making on behalf of incapacitated adults in the UK (Szerletics 2012). The Percy Commission introduced the principle of presumption in favour of informal, 'voluntary' admission which was incorporated into the Mental Health Act 1959. The 1959 Act also established the Mental Health Review Tribunal which would review a detention which had already taken place.

In 1979, (in the case of *Winterwerp v The Netherlands*) the European Court of Human Rights handed down guidance as to the criteria which must be met in order for a 'person of unsound mind' within the definition of Article 5.1(e) to be lawfully deprived of their liberty. These criteria can be found in both the Mental Health Act 1983 sections which authorise deprivation, and the Mental Capacity Act 2005 provisions, which authorise deprivation of liberty. The Winterwerp Criteria established that:

- The mental disorder must be established by an objective body of medical expertise.

- The disorder must be of a kind or degree which warrants compulsory detention.

- Detention must be a necessary and proportionate response.

- For the detention to continue, the mental disorder must persist.

The decision of the ECHR meant that the UK government had to legislate to create a procedure which authorised the deprivation of liberty of those people who lacked the capacity to consent to admission to a place of care and treatment and were not able to leave. The state could no longer rely, as it had done until then, on Section 131 of the Mental Health Act 1983, together with the common law doctrine of necessity.

In 2005, new provision providing for those lacking capacity to make decisions was enacted with the passing into law of the Mental Capacity Act 2005. The purpose of this Act was: (1) to assist people to make decisions where they could; (2) to set out the law as to what should happen if they could not; (3) to create a mechanism whereby decisions could be made in advance of incapacity; (4) to create a role for people who had no one to advocate for them (the Independent Mental Capacity Advocate); and (5) to provide legal protection from being sued for those professionals using the Act properly. However, the Mental Capacity Act did not provide powers to authorise deprivation of liberty and did not address the issues identified in the case of *HL v The United Kingdom*, the so-called Bournewood Gap. The UK House of Lords considered the case of HL, an autistic man who was unable to consent, but did not resist his admission to hospital for care and treatment of his mental health. The medics who were treating him chose to regard HL's lack of obvious objection as meaning he had been admitted on a voluntary basis, so they did not apply the Mental Health Act 1983. However, as he lacked capacity to consent this could not be the case, leaving him without any form of advocacy or judicial oversight and redress. From the perspective of his carers, their family member had been taken from them and was now missing (EHRC 2016). The House of Lords did not consider the extent to which the level of restriction that HL experienced constituted a deprivation of his liberty, but rather considered under common law the extent to which a detention for reasons of medical treatment was 'necessary'. During the House of Lords hearing, evidence was presented that 22,000 additional people would be detained under the Mental Health Act 1983 in any given day – 48,000 each year – if the Lords found in favour of HL. HL's carers took their complaint to the European Court of Human Rights (ECtHR). The ECtHR unanimously concluded that in the case of *HL v UK* (2004) a violation of Article 5(1) had taken place as between 22 July and 29 October 1997, HL was subject to 'continuous supervision and control and was not free to leave' (para 19). HL was therefore deprived of his liberty within the meaning of Article 5(1), without the safeguard of a legal process for a court to review the lawfulness of the detention in contravention of Article 5(4). Their finding was significant as it exposed a gap in the law which was not addressed by the newly incoming mental capacity legislation, that where a person lacked capacity to consent but was not objecting, no powers existed to enact legal safeguards to ensure speedy judicial review of the case.

Just two years on from the Bournewood case, UK law was changed with the Mental Health Act 2007. The Act both amended the Mental Health Act 1983 and introduced the Deprivation of Liberty Safeguards (DoLS) as an amendment to the Mental Capacity Act 2005. Section 64(5) of the Mental Capacity Act 2005 referenced that the definition of a deprivation within the Act was within the meaning of Article 5(1) ECHR; however, it did not define what constituted a deprivation. Determination of whether or not a deprivation was occurring was left as a matter for the courts to consider, taking into account the *nature, duration, effects and manner of execution* of the restriction as ruled in *Engel v The Netherlands* (1976). Best Interest Assessors (BIAs) relied on emerging case law to provide guiding principles when considering the *degree and intensity* of a restriction, *Guzzardi v Italy* (1980), to determine whether it constituted a deprivation. As a result in 2009, the first year of the DoLS, only 536 authorisations were granted (HSCIC 2013), 8 per cent of the number of applications received and a tenth of the level anticipated in the Department of Health Impact Assessment (DH 2008).

As noted by Baker J in *CC v KK* EWHC 2136 (2012)

> Professionals and the court must not be unduly influenced by the 'protection imperative'; that is, the perceived need to protect the vulnerable adult... There is a risk that all professionals involved with treating and helping that person – including, of course, a judge in the Court of Protection – may feel drawn towards an outcome that is more protective of the adult and thus, in certain circumstances, fail to carry out an assessment of capacity that is detached and objective.

In 2014, the Official Solicitor took the cases of *P v Cheshire West and Chester Council* and *P & Q v Surrey County Council* (2011) to the Supreme Court. P was an adult born with cerebral palsy and Down's syndrome who lived with his mother in her home. P and Q (otherwise known as MIG and MEG) were sisters aged 15 and 16 with a learning disability. MIG lived with a foster carer; MEG lived in a residential care home. The Court of Appeal had previously upheld a Court of Protection ruling that in P & Q's (MIG and MEG) best interests, should they try to leave their places of residence they would be restrained. With reference to MIG and MEG, Lord Justice Munby in the Court of Appeal overturned a previous ruling, which determined that the level of restraint and intervention experienced by P constituted a deprivation of his right to liberty, stating the 'relative normality' of P's life had to be established compared with other disabled people with a condition of a similar nature.

The Supreme Court, led by Lady Justice Hale, went back to the European Court of Human Rights ruling on the Bournewood case and challenged the 'tacit' presumption of the 'voluntary' patient. Observing the 'universal character of human rights, founded on the inherent dignity of all human beings', the Court 'rejected' the concept of relative normality. Lady Hale noted that the *HL v UK* case provided an 'acid test' against which all other cases should be considered, that of the person being subject to continuous supervision and control and not being free to leave.

However, as Lord Mostyn observed in *Rochdale Metropolitan Borough Council v KW & Ors* (2014), the implication of the Supreme Court ruling was a dramatic widening of the scope of Article 5(1), with potentially thousands of people subject to unauthorised deprivations of liberty. The number of requests for authorisation since the ruling has increased tenfold (HSCIC 2013). The Law Commission (2015) has proposed changes to simplify the arrangements going forward. Significantly, the other consequence is that Article 5(4) is also engaged, bringing the right of review for an adult lacking capacity and subject to a restriction before an independent body, upholding the principles first envisioned in the Magna Carta and the *positive obligations* as ruled in *Stanev v Bulgaria* (2012) on the UK as a party to the UN Convention on the Rights of Persons with Disabilities, which we will come back to later.

The 2007 amendment to the Mental Health Act 1983 also introduced the role of the Approved Mental Health Professional (AMHP). The AMHP role has the responsibility to coordinate mental health assessment and demonstrate the guiding principles of the Mental Health Act Code of Practice 2008 through upholding principles of least restrictive practice and participation. In preparing this chapter, we asked three social workers why they chose to become AMHPs. All three spoke of feeling a burning sense of injustice about what they were seeing happening to people within the mental health system as driving their decision making. That burning desire to change the world they were seeing just wouldn't go away; in fact, it became more intense with each new person whose circumstances they learned about. They described how they were faced, on almost a daily basis, with experiences of people's human rights being ignored and, in some instances, abused and felt that they needed the power to be able to do something about it. They talked about the people who had inspired them, including the woman who had been in the care system, had been sexually abused by older men and had fallen pregnant when she was 16. Services had sectioned her, and then moved her into a low secure unit where she was told she was not free to leave. Seventeen years later, after her daughter had been removed from her, she was still living in the unit 'for her own protection'. They also talked about the 26-year-old who had started a fire ten years previously, but had never started any fires since. Instead of going down the traditional criminal justice route, he had been admitted on a so-called 'voluntary' basis to hospital. The hospital admission had been extended and extended for an indefinite period of time. He had no release date agreed and commissioners were arguing over who would pay for him once he finally 'stepped down' rather than trying to sort out options to get him home.

Used incorrectly, the Mental Health Act 1983 has the potential to be more restrictive than the criminal justice system, which has automatic safeguards built in such as an end date to any sentence. Section 117 of the Mental Health Act, the aftercare duty, gives professionals the right to remain in people's lives indefinitely. Imagine not being able to move on and leave behind the mistakes of your past despite there being no evidence of another incident happening. Imagine being told that medical professionals know you better than you know yourself, better than your family knows you. Imagine you have a stay in hospital, and when you are discharged you find yourself forever monitored, reviewed, assessed and under threat of another admission if you are deemed to be non-compliant.

Here is an example of where you might see some of these issues in your practice as a social worker. Imagine that you have been asked to support a person who has been detained under a section of the Mental Health Act in a hospital hundreds of miles from their family. The person is described to you by the doctor who makes the referral as having a 'mild learning disability' (what does this actually mean?). When you make contact with the person, you find out that they have been locked up in a hospital for over ten years. As you ask more questions you start to find out more things which at first worry you and eventually start to make you angry about their rights.

You find out that had they been convicted of a minor offence for the reason which resulted in them being detained under the Mental Health Act, the conviction would have been spent by now. They have patiently sat through regular multi-disciplinary team reviews and tribunals. Yet despite all this professional intervention nothing has changed since they were first detained. They are on a concoction of psychiatric medication to stop any natural behaviours, feelings or emotions sneaking out. They are deemed to be a continuing high risk by the clinical team, who recommend a lot more work before they are ready for release. In practice, this means they attend a course one day a week which involves taking a walk around the grounds. When you meet the person face to face you find that this person who the forms describe as being highly risky is intelligent, articulate, and shows insight into what had happened and why. They ask you why they cannot go out more, be closer to their family, and prepare for leaving the hospital and moving on. They sum up their circumstances better than any of the 'professionals' involved – 'I'm 30 and I'm spending the best years of my life in here with people I do not want to be with, away from my family, for what reason?'

Our experience is that people really struggle to understand the legislation they can find themselves subject to through social care and mental health services. The roles of the BIA and the AMHP are crucial in that they authorise legal safeguards to help people challenge the level of restriction imposed on them. The fifth statutory principle of the Mental Capacity Act 2005 and the first guiding principle of the Mental Health Act Code of Practice 2008 are the same: any intervention taken on behalf of a person must be the least restrictive intervention. We argue that what this means is that any action taken by social workers must make life better for that person rather than upholding the status quo of their lives, no matter how much pressure you are put under by concerned friends, family, nurses and GPs. Some rights-based social workers struggle with the potentially oppressive powers which they hold as professionals, interpreting caveats to human rights which for over 200 years have been dominated by the views of doctors applying a clinical/medical lens to people (Kinney 2009). Our argument is that far from the role of BIA or AMHP being in contradiction with rights-based practice, the role of safeguarding human rights is the central organising principle of what social work values stand for. The purpose of these roles are not the deprivation of a person's liberty or authorising enforcing compulsory detentions and admissions to hospital as a way of managing perceived risks (Buckland 2014). Rather their function is to uphold the person's rights, to ensure that any action is necessary and proportionate and that all legal safeguards, including statutory advocacy and speedy judicial review, are in place. Social workers being right in the heart of decisions, challenging the medical view of people being a risk to themselves and others, positions the profession perfectly to prevent significant injustice by advocating for and upholding people's rights and challenging assumptions and oppressive and risk-averse practices. It gives social workers the opportunity for early involvement and for seeking out alternatives to give people a chance at living the life they want to live.

The Mental Health Act Code of Practice 2008 is explicit in stating that all decisions must be compliant with human rights legislation. Understanding of the Mental Health Act (1983) (amended 2007) and its interface with the Mental Capacity Act 2005 when someone lacks capacity but doesn't actively object to the detention (or where because the person has a learning disability professionals assume they lack capacity to make a decision that professionals deem to be 'wise') is particularly poor. The Act was not designed to control people and the guiding principles should always be the starting point for both the Mental Capacity and Mental Health Acts. Challenging this system is not easy; the system is powerful. But whilst detention is the ultimate infringement of someone's liberty, it shouldn't mean their rights, wishes and feelings are deemed irrelevant and ignored; rather, social work has a significant contribution to make to ensure they remain central.

Justice

It is over 100 years since Josiah Wedgewood argued in 1918, whilst campaigning against the draconian Mental Retardation Act, that 'our object... is to secure justice for everybody', yet it feels like we are long way from human rights being universally applied when families and their supporters still have to fight for the rights of their family members to be upheld. On 4 July 2013, Connor Sparrowhawk, aged just 18, experienced an epileptic seizure whilst in an NHS Southern Health Trust bath. Connor, known to his family as Laughing Boy (LB), drowned. The subsequent inquest ruled that LB's death was contributed to by neglect. Five years after Connor died, on 26 March 2018, the Health and Safety Executive won its case against the Trust, with the judge imposing a fine of £1,050,000. In his opening remarks, the judge commented on how regrettable it was that it had taken a family-led campaign to shine a light on the neglect Connor had experienced, which contributed to his death, never giving up on questioning or critically challenging on behalf of Connor. For supporters of the #JusticeForLB campaign, which formed around Connor's family to fight for his right to justice, the judgment was a landmark moment, a culmination of the sadness, tears, trauma, colour, light and laughter described by Connor's mum, Sara Ryan, in her book *Justice for Laughing Boy* (2018), from a collective effort which is perhaps unprecedented. And yet, as Sara observed in her blog, 'none of it will bring back our beautiful boy'.

On 13 March 2017, the Law Commission published their report on Mental Capacity and the Deprivation of Liberty (Law Commission 2017). The overdue report finally arrived a week after news broke of the death of Rusi Stanev, aged 61. The ruling on *Stanev v Bulgaria* ECHR 46 by the European Court of Human Rights in 2012 was the catalyst which led just two years later to what became known as 'the acid test' to determine what would constitute someone being deprived of their liberty. In her landmark Supreme Court Ruling on the Deprivation of Liberty Safeguards, which has come to be known as Cheshire West, Lady Hale referenced the Stanev case in setting the benchmark against which all other cases should be considered, that of the person being subject to continuous supervision and control and not being free to leave. The Law Commission recommended that the DoLS be repealed and set out a replacement scheme which they called the Liberty Protection Safeguards. The UK government brought forward these proposals in the Mental Capacity (Amendment) Bill 2017–2019.

The Cheshire West ruling was a wake-up call to adult social work. We argue it reminded the profession of its roots as a practice-based profession and an academic discipline that promotes social change and development, social cohesion, and the empowerment and liberation of people based on principles of social justice and human rights (IFSW 2014). A common confusion is that the DoLS scheme is not there to deprive a person of their liberty. The DoLS provide for a set of legal safeguards on behalf of the person to protect them by ensuring their right to speedy judicial review against the agency who is depriving them of their liberty. The Cheshire West ruling serves as a reminder to social work that the most important letter in the Deprivation of Liberty Safeguards is the S, which stands for Safeguards. The social worker is the Safeguard, protecting the person's right to experience dignity, equality and liberty and where for their own safety or the safety of others, restrictions are necessary and proportionate, ensuring access to advocacy and speedy judicial review and lifting of those restrictions if the circumstances change.

There is a danger that, as Justice Baker in observed *CC v KK* (2012), the 'protection imperative' may result in professionals treating the person as unable to make a decision just because they perceive that decision to be 'unwise'; however, the right to make unwise decisions is enshrined in statute in Principle 3, Section 1 of the Mental Capacity Act 2005. The purpose of social work and social care commissioning is not to wrap the person in cotton wool in the name of adult protection, but to enable people to experience life in the same way anyone else would.

Conclusion

In this chapter we have argued that integrating human rights within your own practice is entirely, and intrinsically, consistent with your social work values of promoting social justice. Rights-based practice embraces core social work values of anti-discriminatory practice, promotion of autonomy and self-determination, and respect for non-conformity and diversity of thought and belief. To further develop a rights-based approach towards your own practice you need to:

- fully commit to informing individuals of their rights within the law; for example, the right to seek legal advice, the right to challenge decisions and access advocacy

- refuse to be part of any 'professionals meeting' that doesn't include the person

- where appropriate, support and arrange for independent advocacy and interpretation to help the person be involved and understand so that they can communicate their wishes, feelings and beliefs

- become involved in campaigns which advocate for people to be able to access information to help them understand and know their rights

- actively support the use of easy-read guides and work collaboratively with user-led organisations in the promotion of legal rights in all areas of life, including subjects such as voting.

What happens next is the individual's choice, but crucially they will be in control of making the decision.

Social workers need to invest in their post-qualifying professional development if they are to maintain the standards of good-quality social work practice. We argue this should include:

- in-depth knowledge of human rights law, including Articles 5 and 8 of the European Convention on Human Rights

- the practical application of the five statutory principles of the Mental Capacity Act 2005 and the role of case law in defining and shaping case-based reasoning

- development of an in-depth knowledge of the process of selecting least restrictive options when considering best interests decision making

- upholding and promoting the importance of factors such as happiness, and past and present wishes and feelings

- understanding of the role and function of the Court of Protection in practice

- being able to identify when legal advice needs to be sought and the Court of Protection engaged.

If you are to be effective, you need to properly enable risk and tackle where it is being talked up and used as justification for unnecessary and disproportionate responses. Risk is a part of life; it is part of growing and learning. Make risk a positive thing. Find out about risk enablement panels which are developing across the country and consider if this would work for your team or service. In doing so, recognise and celebrate your own humanity and the risks that you have taken which have shaped your life and experience. Making an unwise decision is something we all do. It is part of being human. Build an unwise decision wall and celebrate being part of humanity. Learning by experiences which others think are wrong, risky or unsafe is part of life and how our lives are enriched. Be that social worker who makes life better.

And finally – never forget that social workers are not a form of social police. Safeguarding doesn't mean you have legal powers. Remember that Section 42 of the Care Act 2014 is a duty to make inquiries only. The Guiding Principles and Code of Practice to the Mental Health Act 1983, the Statutory Principles and Code of Practice to the Mental Capacity Act 2005 and the Human Rights Act 1998 provide the legal framework within which social work operates. The S stands for Safeguard. That means the S stands for *you*: you, the social worker, are the safeguard. It is your job to safeguard people's right to have their inherent dignity recognised and their right to liberty and to experience freedom upheld.

Suggested further reading and resources

The reading below (recommended by Luke Clements) offers the reader a comprehensive guide to community care law. The Matt Graham and Jackie Cowley book is a good introduction to working with the Mental Capacity Act in practice. We have also recommended Sara Ryan's book about the colour, joy and love that her son Connor Sparrowhawk brought into her life.

Clements, L. (2017) *Community Care and the Law*. London: LAG Education and Service Trust Limited.

Graham, M. and Cowley, J. (2015) *A Practical Guide to the Mental Capacity Act 2005: Putting the Principles of the Act into Practice*. London: Jessica Kingsley Publishers.

Ryan, S. (2018) *Justice for Laughing Boy: Connor Sparrowhawk – A Death by Indifference*. London: Jessica Kingsley Publishers.

🐱 You are the social worker: Asha

Telephone call from Valery the manager of Green Fields Care Home: 'Asha has lashed out at another resident and her behaviours are becoming difficult to manage.'

Asha has a learning disability and has lived within residential care since the age of 16. The health commissioning manager has decided to move Asha to a 'specialist' care home. Asha has an eating disorder; her support is centred around managing this and helping her to maintain her health. The new care home is a specialist in managing eating disorders. Asha has been assessed as lacking capacity to make decisions about residence and care and treatment previously. As a result, all decisions have been made on her behalf without her involvement. Asha is very close to her mum. However, her mum is also receiving support from services; professionals have avoided speaking with mum about Asha because of this.

When you visit the care home Asha tells you that she feels people care more about her eating disorder than her. She tells you that she wants to live with her mum and doesn't want to go to the new care home.

A social worker responds:

The person is the starting point for this referral, and then we can move on from there. On first reading the referral my eyes are drawn to 'lived within residential care since the age of 16'. I'm making a mental note to discuss what 'home' means for Asha. Is happiness something she associates with her residence? She wants to live with her mum; that doesn't strike me as an outrageous request, so I would like to probe a bit further with the commissioning manager to see what their position has been in the past and why this hasn't happened. When meeting with Asha I would like to spend as much time with her as I can, if she allows me, so that I can really get to grips with what she wants. Does she want to live with mum or is it the only option that Asha can envisage whilst in residential care? As a social worker I often only hear all the negative things about a person in a referral to the team and sometimes risks are exacerbated in order to justify an intervention that someone wants.

I want to get to know Asha, to hear about her, what strengths she has and what her views on her situation are. I also may be making a leap, but it may be that the root of her frustrations and 'lashing out' are due to her lack of control over really basic things in her life such as where she lives and who she lives with. A strengths-based approach to this situation may be the key to unlocking support for her in the future. There will be a reason she is in the care home; it may or may not be a proportionate response to her care needs. However, if we look at where pursuing a strength-based approach takes us it may be quite different to continuing to commission a placement at a residential care home.

Asha is over 16 so the Mental Capacity Act (2005) is a really key piece of legislation for her. Her capacity has been assessed in the past when she was deemed to lack capacity. However, capacity is time and decision specific so, I would be looking at how she could be enabled to make the decision in question – about where she should live – at this point. If Asha is over the age of 18 then DoLS may have been in place in the past. The DoLS legislation means that she may have been afforded a right to appeal her placement through a lawful process in court. This is dependent on the qualifying criteria being met and the DoLS being granted. Another question I'd be asking is where are Asha's rights in all of this? There is no mention of DoLS or an appeal or her mum's views for that matter. There seem to be a lot of things 'done to' as opposed to 'done with' Asha. A reminder of the 'no decision about me, without me' principle the care home may have heard of feels timely. There are a lot of questions here, but my starting point would be what is preventing Asha from living where she wants to live.

An example comes to mind where there was a disagreement about an individual's capacity to make the decision about where they lived. This case reminds us of the unique role that social workers have in individuals' lives. In this case, the health professional was regarded as a leading expert in the condition that the individual was diagnosed with, a condition which the individual, P, didn't want to discuss because he was embarrassed. Both the BIA and the health professional were therefore unable to discuss the condition with him. The health professional concluded that P lacked capacity, whereas the BIA couldn't conclude that P lacked capacity as she wasn't able to disprove that he had capacity. This is important because it reaffirms the route that the MCA designed for us: Principle 1 states that a person is assumed to have capacity until proven otherwise.

Whether Asha does or does not have capacity should not 'make or break' what the outcome of this is. We should always aim to ensure we have done everything within our power to enable the person to make the decision, but as important is that Asha has her wish to live with her mother and if that is achievable and available, we should move mountains to make that happen.

Chapter 3

Wellbeing, Belonging and Citizenship

ELAINE JAMES, HANNAH MORGAN and ROB MITCHELL

Introduction

We commonly associate wellbeing with the state of being comfortable, healthy or happy. A social model of disability, however, requires that we consider a wider interpretation which recognises that wellbeing also includes how people feel and function on a personal level and within society as a whole (New Economics Foundation 2012), drawing inspiration from the way the disabled people's movement define independent living. Jenny Morris, in her book *Independent Lives?* (1993), argued that the very idea of care and caring is an inappropriate way to talk about the support that disabled people want from community services. She proposed a set of principles that should govern community support, being:

- that all human life is of value

- that anyone, whatever their impairment, is capable of exerting choices

- that people who are disabled by society's reaction to physical, intellectual and sensory impairment, and to emotional distress have the right to assert control over their lives

- that disabled people have the right to fully participate in society.

The significance of wellbeing, in its broadest sense, to achieving health outcomes (Bowling 2017) was formally recognised with the foundation of the World Health Organization in 1948. The constitution of the World Health Organization promoted the idea that to be healthy and well required more than an absence of disease or impairment, but rather that there is a subjective, public, social and emotional aspect to health and wellbeing. The idea of subjective wellbeing has continued as a focus for policymakers attempting to find meaningful ways to both reflect people's feelings, satisfaction and sense of purpose arising from the quality of their lives and to exploit apparent associations between wellbeing and longevity (Steptoe, Deaton and Stone 2014).

The Care Act 2014 introduced a statutory duty which required all local authorities in England to be responsible for promoting wellbeing: 'the general duty of a local authority...in the case of an individual, is to promote that individual's wellbeing'. When considering what is necessary and proportionately in a person's best interest, social work which supports people to have a positive sense of self, purpose and belonging is encouraged by the Care Act. It is taking some time for the shift in policy focus introduced by the Act to be realised in local authority settings. Care management practices in adult social care are deeply embedded and the systems which support them, including IT, corporate services and how financial assessments operate, can all generate reasons used to justify not making change happen quickly. Further, the first reaction of most local authorities was to respond to the Care Act as another transactional care management change, with the key changes which drew attention being how social care was charged for and how financial transactions would be processed between people seeking support and the council. But as local authorities have begun to recognise the more profound changes which the Act heralded, attention has finally focused on the more challenging idea of subjective wellbeing and the duty to promote it. Trying to understand how to translate something subjective like wellbeing into a universal entitlement enforceable by judicial oversight of a statutory duty poses challenges and raises a range of questions. Subjective measures are by nature individual and personal; how would that fit with the regularisation of assessment that care management had imposed on the profession and which fitted well with the regulatory and enforcement culture prevalent within local government? How big a change would this mean for social work practice with adults? Does the form that drives the assessment process allow for the level of flexibility that personalised, subjective wellbeing outcomes would require? Can a function such as local government, which has a big, collective responsibility to the place, be sufficiently flexible to reform around subjective outcomes determined by the person and their natural network of support?

Social workers have intimate access to people's lives – to the small things which are important to them and which they feel make their lives worth living. Small and personal is usually what shapes subjective wellbeing. Eleanor Roosevelt, Chairwoman of the committee of the General Assembly of the United Nations which oversaw the work on the United Nations Declaration on Human Rights, observed on the tenth anniversary of the adoption of the Declaration: 'Where, after all, do universal human rights begin? In small places, close to home – so close and so small that they cannot be seen on any maps of the world… Unless these rights have meaning there, they have little meaning anywhere' (United Nations undated).

Social work centres around human-to-human contact and the experiences of human emotions shaped by perceptions of potential futures and past experiences of natural rights. It is our role to tend to the beacon light that hope provides for by cherishing the value people place in the small things that matter to them. When you dismiss the small, you take the first inexorable step towards people no longer being seen as fully human, following a path which leads to 'serviceland'. Tony Osgood (2006) has written about serviceland, a strange place which exists in social care where casual dismissal of the small things that define a good life has become the norm; where the protection imperative dominates and removing someone from their family and placing them into a place where their voice is unheard and their rights are ignored is deemed to be in their best interest. We find serviceland uncomfortable to read about. It leaves us as commissioners of 'care and support' facing a series of uncomfortable questions. Do we sometimes get confused in social care about the limitations of our legal powers? Do we mistakenly regard social workers as being a form of 'soft police', dressing up interference in people's lives as being a form of safeguarding of people's wellbeing? Do we focus on physical aspects of safety to the detriment of mental wellbeing? And in doing so, do we create the conditions which lead to unhappiness, which lead in a self-perpetuating cycle to more 'challenging behaviour', which can lead to us thinking we need to commission yet more services to meet the very needs we have created? Serviceland is a place of unhappiness. How typical is it of people's experience?

To be in amongst the crowd

ROB MITCHELL AND ELAINE JAMES

Andrew's paper file was too big for a filing cabinet. It was also too big to be scanned onto the system. It was locked in a cupboard. Whenever Andrew was allocated a new social worker, which was often, the cupboard was opened, the file carried out and placed on desk and the new incumbent was told to read the case notes on the system and 'read the file'.

The safeguarding referral from the provider read: 'Andrew refused to go to day care. On arrival at the centre, Andrew had refused to get off the community transport bus. Staff were hurt as they had tried to assist him using the safe holds they had been trained to use as per his Positive Behaviour Support Plan. Allocation is required to work with Andrew, possibly to look to increase provider staffing to two to one.'

The allocation meetings were held every Monday. Mike was the newest member of the team. At 22 years old he was straight out of college and a newly qualified social worker. He hadn't read the huge file on Andrew, but he was eager to get stuck into some real social work, so he said he had read it. He persuaded his team manager to allocate the case to him. Mike became Andrew's sixth social worker. The team manager was wary; she was aware that Andrew's case must always be allocated to an experienced social worker. But there was something about Mike's enthusiasm which was engaging. Maybe a fresh pair of eyes would make a difference. It was worth a go.

When Mike arranged to visit Andrew at the residential care home, he was struck by how many people were waiting for him. The door was answered by two staff members. Mike asked to speak to Andrew but was told he needed to wait for Lorraine, the care home manager. Mike was left waiting in the hall, where he stood shifting awkwardly as yet another staff member appeared to check him out. Moments later Lorraine appeared, and Mike was ushered into the office. Sitting behind her desk, Lorraine was an imposing figure. Mike was told Andrew had been sent home again from day care and the provider was about to give notice. Mike needed to agree to increase staffing hours to support Andrew, otherwise she was worried that her staff just couldn't cope. She didn't want to leave Mike with a problem, but she would have to consider that Andrew needed to move as the care home was just not set up to provide this level of support. Mike found himself feeling anxious when faced with the list of concerns that Lorraine gave him about incident after incident her team had documented. However, he held his nerve and found himself spluttering something out about wanting to get to know Andrew first as this was an initial meeting. Lorraine paused. She said, 'Okay, I will take you to him.' Mike stood at Andrew's bedroom door and took in the scene – Andrew's room was a temple to football. From the wallpaper and the bedding to the posters on the wall, the room was filled with football memorabilia. The lampshade was in the shape of a football. On the wall was a fading poster tracking the progress of teams in the last world cup. The bookshelves were filled with football albums. It was like he was stepping into another world.

Andrew was lying on his bed, eyes wide open and looking up towards a bottle green ceiling. Lorraine introduced Mike to Andrew and took a seat in the corner of the room. Andrew spun around on the bed and sat bolt upright and shouted, 'Do you like football? Who's your favourite player?'

Before Mike could answer, Lorraine spoke. 'Andrew, he's read the file. He knows we are not going to talk about football. We are talking about day care today.'

Mike smiled. 'Yes, sometimes. I used to watch football every Sunday with my dad growing up.'

Andrew's face came to life. 'Do you? Do you? I do. I do. Do you know who my favourite player is?'

Lorraine again interjected. 'Andrew, Mike is here today to talk about what happened at the day centre this week.'

Mike felt he needed to try and take control of the situation. He spoke up. 'No, I do not know, who is your favourite player, Andrew?'

Andrew was by now fidgeting, slightly bouncing on the bed. 'Gary Lineker. He plays for England and Spurs. And that's what I'm going to do. Footballer for England – that's my job. I'll play for England. Look.' Andrew got up and pointed to posters on the wall. Behind the bed were wall-to-wall posters of Gary Lineker in various kits and at various stages of his career. Watching how Andrew came to life as he pulled books from the shelf for Mike to share about the life of Lineker, Mike had a sudden moment of realisation. He knew what the room reminded him of. It was like stepping into the bedroom of his 7-year-old nephew Sam. Andrew, aged 32, talked non-stop about football for the rest of the 45-minute visit. Mike listened intently, knowing full well that there was not likely to be any room in this conversation to talk about day care.

Lorraine had been on the phone to discuss her concerns about the visit with his team manager before Mike managed to return to the office: Mike had wound Andrew up by engaging with the football talk.

Andrew had to be kept calm. Football talk had to be structured. The psychologist and psychiatrist had agreed this. Andrew was in a state of agitation and there were risks to other residents and her staff as a result. No consideration was being given to the need for increased hours.

When his team manager asked Mike about the meeting, he referred to the notes he had made in an anxious attempt to explain himself. It was at that point he realised that he had barely written anything down on his pad apart from the words 'Gary' and 'football, that's my job'. Mike agreed that his next meeting with Andrew would be more structured and would focus on considering the provider's request that they have an authorised increase in hours to up his support to two to one.

However, Mike had not factored in Andrew's feelings about how he wanted the meeting to go. As a result, their next encounter was equally chaotic. This time Mike set up the assessment to take place at the day centre where the incident had allegedly taken place.

Once again Andrew wanted to talk about his love of football. This time he talked about the season cup, which teams were likely to win their leagues, who was facing relegation. Andrew knew every team, their manager and where they currently were in the league table. As it got close to the end of the allocated time for Mike to conclude his assessment, he asked Andrew if he ever got chance to play football. Andrew didn't answer. For the first time Andrew sat quietly with a confused frown on his face. Then he started talking again about the league tables. Mike wondered what he had stumbled upon. As he was leaving the day centre, he took an opportunity and chatted to the staff about Andrew, asking if he ever played football as part of his community activity plan. The staff were surprised by the question; no, they hadn't ever thought of Andrew playing football. They weren't sure how to make that happen. No one else who attended the centre was that interested in playing and they needed to staff the centre, so they couldn't just release staff, unless of course Mike was able to increase their hours so they could provide a Personal Assistant service dedicated to Andrew.

Mike couldn't stop thinking about Andrew when he got home. He realised that he liked Andrew. His enthusiasm for football was infectious. Mike remembered when he was a child and had played in a Sunday league. He'd loved being part of that team. They hadn't been the best team, they usually lost, but the joy of playing with others had kept him going even in the middle of winter. He woke up the next morning with a resolve clear in his mind; he was going to take Andrew to watch a football match.

Mike's team manager was bemused but decided to go with it. She had taken a risk allocating Andrew to Mike, now she needed to trust her instincts and go with it. She told Mike to make sure he had properly logged his risk assessment and that he must get Lorraine to sign the plan off. This took a bit longer. Lorraine was extremely concerned about the boundary issues, but she was prepared to acknowledge that Andrew had been calmer this last month since Mike had started his assessment. She had no objections. Mike made contact with the local club, who were happy to help and told him they had a steward who was trained in disabled access and would support Mike with Andrew on the day.

Lorraine and the team helped Andrew prepare for the day. They bought him a team scarf and hat to wear and made sure he was wrapped up properly. Mike suggested that lunch was a pie at the club, which wouldn't usually be allowed according to Andrew's carefully controlled diet plan, but just this once they agreed. Mike walked with Andrew to the club, with a staff member supporting. Andrew got more and more excited as he started spotting others on their way to the match. 'That's my scarf! You are going too! Who's your favourite player?' he shouted out. He was delighted to find that people reacted and cheered him back, answering his shouts. As they got to the match, they were met by the steward who helped them in through the disabled access entrance. Andrew couldn't take his eyes off the steward. 'I love your jacket. Can I have one?' Andrew and Mike found themselves in the main stands, which were quickly filling. Colour, sound, excitement, noise. Andrew was enthralled. He couldn't take his eyes off the 2000-strong crowd. He turned to Mike and said, 'This is the best day of my life.'

Later that night, Mike sat sifting through his feelings about the day. Reflecting on how it had gone he found himself pondering on what had really happened. Andrew had loved the day, but he hadn't really paid much attention to the actual match. He had become lost in the crowd, the noise, the rapturous cheers when a goal had been scored. There was more to understand about this love of football. Mike decided to take Andrew to the next home match and this time to more critically observe what was going on.

The next match was two weeks away. This time Mike had no problem getting agreement from all concerned. Lorraine was respectful in her conversation with Mike; he was doing a good job. Andrew had never been known to behave so well. She was even considering freeing up some staffing hours to reallocate them to another resident who she was now more concerned about. The day centre was also reporting that Andrew was much more settled than they had seen him in a long time. Mike arranged once again with the stewards to meet at the disabled access entrance. They had liked Andrew, and they invited Mike to arrive early and offered to give Andrew 'a bit of a tour' of the steward's area.

Andrew loved the steward's area the minute he saw it. A small dressing room with facilities for a cuppa. Bright high-visibility uniforms. And then came the big moment that changed Andrew's life. 'Here Andrew, we have got a special treat for you. We have got you your own steward's jacket. Do you want to try it on?' Mike watched in surprise as Andrew reverently held the high vis jacket. He was completely lost for words. The steward asked to speak to Mike. 'We have a community scheme. It is a bit of a kick about, but I think Andrew would be welcome. Shall we set something up?'

Mike turned to Andrew. 'What do you think; do you want to do this Andrew?'

Andrew stood quietly, very carefully handling his jacket. 'Can I wear this?'

'Yes,' was the reply. 'You can be a steward.'

Andrew has been a regular now at the club for over five years. With support from Mike, he has moved on from his residential care home to a supported living flat where he has his own space. Andrew is a football steward for the community programme. Sometimes on big match days he helps out too. Andrew has never been happier. His medication has been reduced, he has lost weight and he has thought about playing. But it is not the game he loves; it is the crowd, being part of something bigger, having people shout replies to him, being noticed and part of the community that is football.

Belonging

National high-profile serious incidents where social workers were involved, such as the circumstances relating to Steven Neary (2011), Winterbourne View (Flynn 2012) and the preventable death of Connor Sparrowhawk (NHS Southern Health 2016), challenge the profession to review its role in balancing the dual outcomes of helping people remain independent and safe. When tragic outcomes are reported they potentially shake the foundation of the long-held professionally 'taken-for-granted assumption' that professional practice is 'helpful' (James, Morgan and Mitchell 2017; Morgan 2012). Dealing with the messy stuff, love, relationships and the need for one human being to have a sense of belonging which is shared with another may feel scary and unsafe for professionals who genuinely believe that their intervention which interferes with the private and family life of the person is in their best interest.

Care management processes, arising from the Community Care reforms of the 1990s, aimed to standardise care and support into a cycle of assessment, support plan, review. Conversely, as Lipsky (2010) contends, standardising of processes leads to people experiencing uneven-handed treatment. Lipsky went further, arguing against the dehumanising effect of the routinising of interactions through the imposition of mass processing within social work in 1980. Mass processing results in disconnection between people and their families. The trade in people (Brown, James and Hatton 2017) between care homes and hospitals which has subsequently emerged has severed any sense of people belonging to a local community. People are left feeling unsettled, unaccepted, dislocated in place and unwanted. It is a system where the professional actively seeks out a medical diagnosis, a mental health condition, the professional comfort of a 'voluntary admission' under the Mental Health Act rather than hold a level of risk which will uphold the person's right not to be displaced and mass processed. Goodley and Runswick-Cole (2014), through their ground-breaking, disruptive work on the iHuman project, have curated a collection which illuminates how the very act of renaming care and support – which is by nature individualistic – as being a 'system' which is uniform in how it serves populations, in itself results in potentially traumatic impacts as disabled people are stripped of their voices, politics and capacity for self-advocacy, instead experiencing systematic dehumanisation. A system becomes a place where belonging, love and human relationships, with all the complexities and messiness that they generate, confuse and confound professionals, who view family members with suspicion and hide behind the convenience of a standardised, mechanistic response. Good social workers will carefully check themselves to make sure that they don't fall into this trap, that they aren't becoming street-level bureaucrats (Lipsky 2010) whose actions to protect people involve taking them way from the very thing that we all strive for: a place where they feel settled, accepted, wanted and loved – a place where they belong.

Observations made of casual attributions of risk towards his son Steven made by Mark Neary in his books telling the story of their lives are a powerful reminder, softly spoken by Mark, of the impact of small things which begin the process of stripping a person of their humanity. Mark recalls how a staff member in the unit where Steven was unlawfully detained had casually referred to Steven as 'a nasty piece of work'. Steven heard this comment being made about him. Years later, Steven remembered the comments. They still had the power to upset him. Such casual attributions of risk are strongly associated with power, authority and control (Clarke *et al.* 2017). The lifetime of distress caused by a passing comment is testimony not only to the power of the spiteful choice of words used to describe a fellow human being, but, moreover, perhaps the intent behind the words. Whether or not the support worker believed the words they used is one thing, but the intent behind the words, the casual hateful remark towards someone they were caring for, is disturbing.

As a social worker, you will have completed a programme of social work education which promotes understanding that words are symbols of the culture of social care. Legitimisation of such casual dismissal of another reflects a culture which thrives on not allowing people to feel settled, accepted or wanted. We are comfortable with belligerence in social care. We can even deal with hate. But if someone feels settled, accepted and wanted there is a risk that they may be loved and that is considered a real risk in social care. It's easier to frame people as something different to us, to despise and dismiss someone as being something other, than it is to consider them as equals in the common human cause, a person with the same desires as you, me and all other human beings. If we consider people who require social care as people like us, it forces us to consider the totality of that. This leads to a risk that people might be possibly be loved. Love and belonging in social care anyone? Love and belonging are words that you very rarely see in assessments and support plans. Rob Mitchell recalls how, during the last few years of her life, his sister used a direct payment to make her own care and support arrangements. It took her a while to find the right person for the role of her personal assistant but eventually she found Christine (not her real name). What amazed Rob at the time was how much his sister felt that she had to hide her relationship with Christine from the social care assessors, reviewing officers and nurses who funded the arrangement. Rob describes his sister as an extremely generous person with a huge personality, her relationships with people being intense and beautiful. Within weeks of employing

Christine, he describes how his sister's personality and humanity had completely dwarfed the direct payment arrangement that was supposed to govern it – it was always going to. Over the years a deep friendship grew but it was always hidden in the shadows of social care. When Christine was diagnosed with cancer it was his sister, the person Christine was paid to care for, who was at the hospital with her holding Christine's hand as she received the diagnosis and prognosis. As Christine died it was his sister who stayed with her, gently singing to her and reassuring her that her daughter would be cared for. After Christine died, his sister became the guardian of her daughter until she was 18. All this, the complexity of the relationship, was extremely normal if you knew Rob's sister and Christine. Humanity had completely overtaken the narrow definition we have of people in social care. That the relationship was kept secret, hidden from the health and social care professionals as they didn't believe any professional would or could ever understand it, should be a matter of shame for those who were involved in their lives. There wasn't an assessment form which allowed for an explanation of the relationship, the love and humanity between them. But there was an assessment of form on boundaries, inappropriate behaviours and people abusing direct payments which might require another form, a safeguarding form – all things that appear to be quite expected of people who need social care. How could that relationship ever be explained to social care with an expectation that the state would understand it? How do you tell an audit officer or a continuing health care nurse or a social worker that a human relationship and love were meeting the 'assessed need' for both the cared for person and the carer?

Lord Justice Munby, in the case *Local Authority X v MM & Anor (No. 1)* (2007) EWHC 2003 (Fam), observed that the very actions we take to keep people safe are often the thing that leads to their lives no longer being lives worth living. In doing so, he contested long-held assumptions about the role of social work and the function of safeguarding duties which social workers perform:

> The fact is that all life involves risk, and the young, the elderly and the vulnerable, are exposed to additional risks

and to risks they are less well equipped than others to cope with. But just as wise parents resist the temptation to keep their children metaphorically wrapped up in cotton wool, so too we must avoid the temptation always to put the physical health and safety of the elderly and the vulnerable before everything else. Often it will be appropriate to do so, but not always. Physical health and safety can sometimes be bought at too high a price in happiness and emotional welfare. The emphasis must be on sensible risk appraisal, not striving to avoid all risk, whatever the price, but instead seeking a proper balance and being willing to tolerate manageable or acceptable risks as the price appropriately to be paid in order to achieve some other good – in particular to achieve the vital good of the elderly or vulnerable person's happiness. What good is it making someone safer if it merely makes them miserable? (para 121)

Citizenship and recognition of rights

The struggle for recognition, *Kampf um Anerkennung*, was proposed by the German philosopher Hegel (1807). Hegel philosophised that the nature of self-consciousness was the recognition of struggle between two individuals for dominance. Nearly 150 years after Hegel, Hannah Arendt similarly argued in her 1951 book, *The Origins of Totalitarianism* (2017), that human rights are mediated through others. Arendt touched on concepts of belonging being central to having recognition. Proposing the phrase, 'the right to have rights' she formulated the concept of human rights being conferred through nation states recognising citizenship, arguing that 'stateless' people therefore had no access to rights. Arendt argued that the process of conferring citizenship status was too important to be left in what she called the 'relic galleries' of an outdated political past. Perhaps the plight of refugees and those seeking political asylum would be a current equivalence to her 'stateless', floating disconnected from a nation state prepared to confer citizenship, and with it access to protections afforded by human rights conventions. Arendt's observations about the plight of the stateless provided evidence to her that human beings did not have rights qua human, but rather that access to those rights was dependent on membership of a community, a political entity which would provide recognition of those rights and safeguard access to them. For Arendt, rights are only rights if they are recognised.

In the context of a sustained, critical debate over recognition of rights, Nancy Fraser and Axel Honneth entered into a rigorous discussion about the nature of social justice. Fraser contends that with the dominance of identity politics, the politics of recognition eclipses wider debates about redistribution of resources which are required to achieve a fair and just society. Fraser provides a convincing argument that oppression is multi-faceted, a position with which Honneth finds common cause. However, they differed in their view on how best to tackle this. Honneth advocated for the quality of the relationship between mother and child being the basis on which self-confidence and self-recognition could be achieved. This idea has strongly resonated through much social work theory. However, Fraser rejected the reductionist approach of citing self-recognition within the social psychology of relationships (Garret 2010), arguing that this path led to the risk of victim blaming. In current times, Sara Ryan in her blog, 'My Daft Life', calls out the repetitiveness with which 'mother-blaming' is experienced by parents of children with disabilities. Fraser's position echoes that of Arendt, reminding us of the importance of mediators in achieving recognition, and of the power that mediators hold over the citizenship-less.

All nation states which have signed and ratified the United Nations Convention on the Rights of Persons with Disabilities (United Nations 2006), which came into force in 2008, are required to guarantee disabled citizens the same rights as non-disabled citizens. The Convention was heralded as having achieved a paradigm shift away from disabled people being considered as objects of charity, with professionals, such as social workers, there to rescue or fix them. As Beckett put it in his novel *Molloy* (2009/1951, p.21): 'against the charitable gesture [of social workers], there is no defence that I know of'. This outdated image of the profession needs to be shaken off once and for all. Social work has a unique specialism. That specialism is upholding human rights and recognition of the inherent dignity of all human beings through a global profession with a global definition of purpose. Recognition of right in the eyes of the global profession of social work does not require the qualification of there being a nation state which decides whether or not to confer citizenship on a person first.

Our experiences in health and social care, however, suggest that positive obligations on signatory nation states to recognise the rights of disabled citizens are only realised where practitioners charged with implementation recognise and safeguard those rights. Social work as a profession, if nothing else, is innately political, is informed by politics, designed by politics, promoted and or changed by politics. We are not suggesting that all social workers have to participate in elections and get out and vote or that they need to have a clear-cut political persuasion. However, it is a precondition for the disabled being recognised as citizens with access to the full range of democratic rights experienced by their non-disabled peers that social workers know the issues and the political world they live and work within, issues that will fundamentally shape the way they work and the lives of the people they work with. The BASW and Shaping our Lives Charter advances the following guiding principles, proposing that social workers will:

- take a rights-based approach – based on the United Nation Convention on the Rights of Persons with Disabilities (UNCRPD), the Equality Act and the Care Act

- promote independent living as the cornerstone of wellbeing

- always value the voice of people with lived experience of disability

- be committed to opposing discrimination and to promoting social justice

- not be satisfied till everyone has full and equal citizenship.

We contend that unless practice is rooted in the social model of disability it will remain inadequate in its response to the barriers and other forms of oppression and discrimination experienced by disabled people. However, it is over 30 years since the social model of disability was proposed by Mike Oliver and since BASW formally adopted the model (Morgan 2012), and yet disabled adults still do not experience the full range of their democratic rights as citizens (Agran and Hughes 2013; Beckman 2007; Kjellberg and Hemmingsson 2013; Political and Constitutional Reform Committee 2014; Redley *et al.* 2012). Social work education has an important role in promoting the social model of disability as a framework for social workers' practice.

Article 13 of the UNCRPD significantly expands the positive obligations local authorities, and by extension social workers acting on their behalf, are charged with: they should promote social justice through upholding values of dignity, equality, democracy and freedom. Signatories to the UNCRPD are required to guarantee disabled citizens the same rights as non-disabled citizens. Despite the global definition for social work making explicit a commitment to upholding human rights being a defining aspect of the profession, many social workers would argue that the imposition of care management approaches, regulatory practice and inspection regimes evidence that there is not a shared perspective that social workers are there to safeguard and uphold a comprehensive programme of enforceable rights for all.

Could understanding of human rights, framed by the UNCRPD, reshape a more human approach towards social work practice that could bridge the gap between the theory of social justice and the practice of people experiencing the full range of their rights as citizens? Article 29 of the UNCRPD requires signatories to guarantee that disabled people have the same right to participate in political and public life as non-disabled citizens. Yet adults with learning disabilities continue to experience discrimination through suggestions that they lack capacity to participate. Analysis suggests that no more than a fifth to a third of adults with a learning disability exercise their democratic right to participate in UK General Elections, a theme we shall return to later (James 2016; James, Harvey and Hatton 2018). There is no mental capacity test in relation to the right to vote. Arguments all seem to relate to a suggestion that adults with a learning disability will make 'unwise decisions' about who to vote for; that they will be unduly manipulated into choosing who they like the look of the most, which will somehow undermine the whole process. That people all over the world have been voting in elections based on who they like the look of the most for generations doesn't seem to enter the minds of 'gatekeepers' who are determined to prevent people who have a learning disability label from exercising the most fundamental of rights to have their voice heard and to influence decision making.

The UK government, as a signatory to the Convention, is required to uphold Article 29 when conducting the election of the UK Parliament, which must take place up to every five years. Who can (and cannot) participate in UK elections and cast a vote is defined by the Representation of the People Acts 1989 and 2000 (Ministry of Justice 1989 and 2000). The Acts state that to qualify to register in UK parliamentary elections a person must be a Commonwealth or Republic of Ireland citizen, who is of voting age and is resident in the constituency. Less than a third of people with learning disabilities voted in the 2001 UK General Election (Emerson and Hatton 2008) compared with 59.4 per cent of the general population (UK Political Info 2016). A study of the 2005 UK General Election found that 16.5 per cent of people with learning disabilities voted (Keeley *et al.* 2008) compared with 61.4 per cent of the general population (UK Political Info 2016). We have found in our own work on democratic rights and participation that these assumptions may be an underestimation of the level of systemic disenfranchisement (James 2016; James *et al.* 2018). A review of the international research into citizenship and democratic participation indicates that whilst a social model of disability has a positive influencing effect on people's belief in their right to participate and sense of belonging as a citizen (Kjellberg and Hemmingsson 2013), attitudes and assumptions of social care support staff in recognising the rights of disabled people were significant barriers to participation (Friedman 2018; Friedman and Rizzolo 2017; Hood 2016; James *et al.* 2018; Lord, Ashley Stein and Fiala-Butora 2014; Willis *et al.* 2016) contributing to democratic exclusion, which is by nature discriminatory and a fundamental breach of people's human rights.

Another example of the potential mind-shift and behaviour change which is required is writ large within UNCRPD Article 14, which provides that 'disability shall in no case justify a deprivation of liberty'. This should challenge all our thinking in social care about the framing of the Mental Health Act Amended 2007 which still includes autism and learning disability as a legal basis for detention.

Case law, which has helped BIAs post-Cheshire West in applying the Mental Capacity Act 2005, has absolutely clarified that having a clinician tell you that you are on the autistic spectrum (which by definition means it covers everyone) or have a learning disability (does anyone even know what this actually means?) is not a legal basis for authorisation of a person's liberty to be deprived. In addition, Article 23 provides that 'in no case shall a child be separated from parents on the basis of disability of either the child or one or both of the parents'. The genius of the UNCRPD and the Mental Capacity Act is that as 'professionals' we can no longer use a characteristic associated with a clinical label to justify poor decision making.

For health professionals trained in clinical autonomy perhaps UNCPD Article 15 – 'no one shall be subjected without his or her free consent to medical or scientific experimentation' – is the most difficult for them to reconcile their professional training with. Case law emerging from the Court of Protection consistently upholds that the person's wishes, feelings and beliefs must be heard and upheld as central to decision making. So-called 'unwise decisions', which are the very central tenet of 'sparkling lives' filled with light, colour and happiness, should be our ambition in social care, not safe, protected and ultimately dull lives.

King's College Hospital NHS Foundation Trust v C & Anor [2015] EWCOP 80, [2015] MHLO 125

> The question in this difficult and finely balanced case is whether C has the capacity to decide whether or not to consent to the life saving treatment that her doctors wish to give her following her attempted suicide, namely renal dialysis. Without such treatment the almost inevitable outcome will be the death of C. If the treatment is administered the likelihood is that it will save C's life, albeit that there remains an appreciable and increasing possibility that C will be left requiring dialysis for the rest of her life. C now refuses to consent to dialysis and much of the treatment associated with it... For the reasons set out above I am not satisfied on the evidence before the court that the Trust has established on the balance of probabilities that C lacks

capacity to decide whether or not to accept treatment by way of dialysis... [A] capacitous individual is entitled to decide whether or not to accept treatment from his or her doctor. The right to refuse treatment extends to declining treatment that would, if administered, save the life of the patient and, accordingly, a capacitous patient may refuse treatment even in circumstances where that refusal will lead to his or her death. The decision C has reached to refuse dialysis can be characterised as an unwise one. That C considers that the prospect of growing old, the fear of living with fewer material possessions and the fear that she has lost, and will not regain, 'her sparkle' outweighs a prognosis that signals continued life will alarm and possibly horrify many, although I am satisfied that the ongoing discomfort of treatment, the fear of chronic illness and the fear of lifelong treatment and lifelong disability are factors that also weigh heavily in the balance for C. C's decision is certainly one that does not accord with the expectations of many in society. Indeed, others in society may consider C's decision to be unreasonable, illogical or even immoral within the context of the sanctity accorded to life by society in general. None of this however is evidence of a lack of capacity. The court being satisfied that, in accordance with the provisions of the Mental Capacity Act 2005, C has capacity to decide whether or not to accept treatment C is entitled to make her own decision on that question based on the things that are important to her, in keeping with her own personality and system of values and without conforming to society's expectation of what constitutes the 'normal' decision in this situation (if such a thing exists). As a capacitous individual C is, in respect of her own body and mind, sovereign.

Conclusion

In this chapter we have argued that a person's sense of wellbeing is entangled with their sense of being accepted and belonging to their community. We argue that social work transcends being merely agents of the state; it is an international profession with a global identity. Thus, social workers have a role in securing justice for those who are 'state-less', to uphold the inherent dignity of all people and ensure universal access to the full range of human rights. We have explored the positive obligations which signatory states to the UNCRPD must uphold, arguing that the UNCRPD provides a transformative framework for practice which elevates social work interventions beyond the limitations of care management systems. Further, we have argued that once you are a subject of the trade of people which occurs between health and social care, services divorce connections between natural networks of support from family and community leading to isolation and increasing the risk of abuse and harm occurring. Good social work tackles this structural discrimination by remaining focused on the person and encouraging creative support planning which reconnects people to the networks they belong to, and by promoting active citizenship.

Suggested further reading and resources

Adams, R., Dominelli, L. and Payne, M. (eds) (2019) *Practising Social Work in a Complex World.* London: Red Globe Press.

Arendt, H. (2017) *The Origins of Totalitarianism.* Later Edition Reprint. London: Penguin.

Osgood, T. (2006) 'Still Hurting: What Jane Did Next' Serviceland, Commissioning & Monitoring: A Triad of Impairments. Accessed on 04/03/2019 at http://tonyosgood.com/wp-content/uploads/2017/04/Still-Hurting-What-Jane-Did-Next.pdf

iHuman, Disruptive Research into what it means to be Human. http://ihuman.group.shef.ac.uk/

🐱 You are the social worker: Robert

Robert is a 22-year-old man with learning disabilities who lives within a supported living house.

Robert says he is looking to move out and live independently. However, the supported living team is not keen on this idea and feel he would be very unsafe. Their main anxieties are that Robert is vulnerable and likely to be exploited by others. The team also report that Robert has not made the most of college opportunities and has refused to go on supported employment training.

Robert frequently absconds from the group home and is known to spend some of his time in local pubs where he has gambled money playing cards and has got drunk frequently, on one occasion ending up in hospital.

Robert reports that his mobile phone has been confiscated by his supported living carers as there were concerns that he was using his phone to arrange to meet with a girl who they think is exploiting him. Robert describes the girl as being his girlfriend.

Robert is skilled in buying and selling electrical goods at the market. He also likes to run car boot sales with his dad at times. He likes to spend time at the rugby with his mum and is known to the ground staff at the club. On one memorable occasion Robert sold half-time raffle tickets. Robert tells people he works for the club.

Robert's supported living carers are bringing the case to your attention. They feel the risks are unmanageable and that they need an increase in their hours so that they can increase the staffing levels to support Robert.

A social worker responds:

There is a lot of information in this scenario that is concerning in relation to the care provider. However, the role of the social worker in working effectively with Robert is to remain focused on keeping him at the centre of things, helping enhance his status as a citizen and not becoming distracted by poor practice of the support providers – at least not to start with and not without Robert's consent.

I think the 'hook' with this case is for the social worker to concentrate on what Robert likes and what it is that provides him with self-worth. Therefore, Robert's interest in rugby and buying and selling goods would be a great place to frame discussions with him. If these are the things that enthuse him, then that's the place to start. Through building up a relationship with Robert around these issues the social worker is far more likely to get buy-in from him to discuss the more difficult aspects of his life, if Robert permits that. And it is likely that supporting Robert to build on his likes will far more likely enable him to experience what most people want in life, which is often reported as relationships, occupation, housing and hope. How much of our relationships, occupation and subsequent housing are interlinked and provide us with a level of security to flourish from and grow? Wolfensberger's social role valorisation theory (1983) is a concept that provides social workers with a great framework from which to work with people. The theory states that the good things in life which most of us desire are far more easily accessible to those in society who have valued social roles. Within Robert's life there is little in the way of valued social status. He has no housing other than what is provided to him due to his social care needs, he has no employment and he is experiencing difficulties maintaining relationships as a consequence of poor social care provision. The job of the social worker is to work with Robert so that he gets to join 'the club'.

For some people the world of social care does far more damage than it does good and that may be the case for Robert. Why would anyone choose to live with rules around them that are not essentially fair or equitable? It's a fundamental human right. Therefore, in Robert's case his social care needs (if he has any) may be best seen to be separate from the traditional approach and support that he has. A housing support unit that feels someone exerting their liberty to leave the home (and the social worker would rightly make the assumption that Robert has capacity to make the decision of course) as 'absconding' is probably unlikely to see Robert as a full citizen. Given that they do not recognise this human right then it is highly unlikely that they will accept Robert's desire for a relationship, job and hope for the future.

In the pursuit of social justice, I think it is possible that social workers may lose sight of the person and concentrate their efforts on correcting the behaviours of those they feel have erred, who in this case would be the provider. However, there is an inherent danger here in that the social worker adopts the hero mantle, invariably without the consent of the person, and this results in the social worker being able to rectify unlawful behaviours or bad practice but not necessarily enabling the person to experience their freedoms.

Chapter 4

Love, Hope and Relationships

ELAINE JAMES and ROB MITCHELL

Introduction

In the run up to Valentine's Day, given the time of year, it was perhaps unsurprising that our thoughts were filled with love and relationships. Talk around the social work office was full of tales of flowers and cards and chocolates. Some were proud of how much thought they had put into getting the best possible gift for their partner. Others were perhaps even more proud of how little thought (and money) they were planning to get away with. All the office conversations had a theme in common, however: the assumption that these couples only had each other to be accountable to. At no point did the thought pass anyone's mind that they might need permission from someone else to show their feelings, spend money on a present and spend time with the person they loved. This assumption was thrown into stark contrast at a meeting we had with self-advocates that week. The group included a couple who had been together for years and wanted to get married. They had planned to propose to each other this Valentine's Day. Listening to them explain that they had been told by the people who controlled their money, their tenancy agreements and, it would appear, their lives, that they could get married 'in another three years' time, if their relationship worked out over the long term' was heartbreaking.

For the Valentine's I'll never know

ROB MITCHELL

There's a song by a band called the Wedding Present which, like so many other songs, is about falling in love. However, this song is about that moment when you meet someone for the first time where your stomach spins, you cannot eat, you cannot sleep and yet despite this, as the lyric goes, you 'cannot even remember the colour of her eyes'. The song talks about that first fleeting moment of a returned smile, of bursting out with laughter on the walk home together and of subsequent endless telephone calls to each other (it was written in the mid-1980s). It's about that mad bit. The bit where the risk has paid off, even if it's only momentarily.

I know it's different for everybody, but that song has always resonated with me because that is how it feels when it happens. It's a kind of prolonged Christmas Eve of anticipation. It's mystifying, scary and the most exhilarating experience that you can have. It's the pay-off from taking a massive risk. It's the 1000 to 1 off-chance of a new human relationship that may lead to love and will probably start with lust and may definitely, hopefully, include some happiness somewhere along the journey. The risks you've taken have been huge. The smile that might be unrequited, the humiliation of a misread signal, the shocking uncomfortableness of a blind date from hell, the most personal feeling of rejection if, as may be likely, a rejection is just around the corner. Yet despite that, despite all of that, you felt it was a risk worth taking.

Love and falling in love, seeing people fall in and out of love, and the beginning and ending of relationships play a huge part in our lives. I've completed two courses at university, seven years of my life spent studying humanity in social care, and I've completed countless additional training courses, but I genuinely cannot recall ever writing the word 'love' in one single assignment that I have completed. I have definitely never written the word in an exam. I cannot remember a single lecture on love or certainly not one that didn't medicalise it or quickly talk of love in terms of 'attachment' or 'obsession'. But love and relationships appear to be clear things that drive us. Even if we do not choose love or are not loved it seems to me to be an active thought, if sometimes a terribly sad one for many people. It's a thing. It's a part of us. But we do not really get close to it when it comes to health and social care.

In terms of the work we do as social workers you would think that we are the profession to help with this where people want support – it's sort of in our job title. But in my career in social care I have found the most significant block in terms of our thinking about supporting people to experience love, risks and all. In terms of people with learning disabilities I can count on the fingers of one hand the number of conversations I have had with people where there has been a positive approach to helping someone with any aspect of having that Wedding Present song feeling. I hear about sex a lot. And sexually transmitted infections. And grooming. The words 'sex and relationships' in social care are invariably linked to risk and danger, rarely love. I worked with a young man some years ago who according to his allocated learning disability nurse had had sex with his boyfriend, who also had a learning disability, after an evening party at the day centre. Within the course of that day over 20 professionals became aware of what had happened. We knew where it happened and more or less what happened. The police were mentioned. No crime had taken place, but someone thought something needed to be done. What about the risks? What about consent? What about protection? Everyone focused on the sex. No one of course said anything about love. Whilst I find the term 'making love' a bit toe-curling, it was safe to say that none of the people who got to hear the intimate details of whatever happened between that loving couple stopped for one moment to consider it to be anything other than a physical act. The couple are still together. They are still upsetting people by having sex. No one is mentioning that they love each other and may get married. No one is talking about how their lives have been enhanced through love. The fact that as a couple they feel they want to stay in each other's company all day every day and have largely rejected social care and choose to catch the bus to the seaside and 'skip' the day centre seems to anger professionals rather than be celebrated. But surely that's what love does; it puts everything else outside of that relationship into context. For them, love is the answer, not social care. It makes perfect sense that that would be the outcome. Social care, day centres, endless games of ten pin bowling, coffee and cake in Merry England for ten people and two carers – all makes sense when there's nothing in your life other than people who are paid to care for you, especially if you also do not have the comfort of love from your family. Add love into the mix and suddenly 'outcomes' and 'achievable goals' and 'support plans' find their context – in the bin. Love between two people contextualises everything, including health and social care. Is the reason why we dress the possibility of love up for the people we support in terms of risk and danger, risks that we are nonetheless willing to take ourselves and not infrequently do so, but ensure it remains always just outside of reach and relevance of those we support, due to the context it puts us in? If we understand love and humanity, we have to understand our place somewhere way down in the pecking order. Our rules, our say so, our plans for you suddenly lose gravitas when competing with forces like love. What always strikes me about Mark and Steven Neary's powerful account about 'Getting Steven Home'(2011) is that via the Court of Protection the local authority seem very late in the day to be forced into having to grudgingly accept the fact that there is a relationship between Mark and Steven which must be respected and upheld in law (Article 8) but never really seem to get close to understanding that it is the love between them that drives everything about their words, actions and motives. It's as if love is quite literally an emotion beyond us. We have typed 'love' into our health and social care computers and it's come back with an error message and then crashes.

So we tend to stick with what we know and what keeps us safe. We have sort of come up with a fudged thing in assessments which is about relationships. This means that we do not really have to talk about love, but we can talk about other people – significant others, next of kin, nearest relatives and relevant persons. And we have got a form and a process for every relationship. Some relationships (nearest relative and relevant person) even come with special powers. Whether the nearest or relevant relationship is loving never really crosses our minds. Love becomes relationships. Relationships become processes. Processes get processed. Health and social care boxes are ticked. Love does not live here any more. Not that it ever did.

The courts have ruled that happiness is a relevant factor for social workers to consider, as it is part of a determination as to whether care and support is in someone's best interest. In the case of P & Q, also known as MIG and MEG, LJ Wilson observed that happiness was a condition of deprivation of liberty safeguard authorisation being lawful:

> Is happiness relevant? Although a feature which overlaps with happiness is in my view relevant – see [25] below – I agree with the submissions on behalf of P and Q and of the Commission that a person's happiness, as such, is not relevant to whether she is deprived of her liberty. Its relevance is as to whether any such deprivation is in her best interests: see s.4(6)(a) of the Mental Capacity Act 2005. Such is a necessary condition of its being 'lawful' and thus of its not infringing Article 5.

Intimate lives

A few months ago, a social worker told us about a man called Peter (not his real name) that she had been asked to meet with and support. Peter lived in a shared house with other people. He lacked the capacity to consent to where he should live for the purposes of care and treatment. Her involvement related to a request to authorise the decision that he continued to live there. She told us how, when she met with Peter, what really stood out to her was the intimacy of his relationship with balloons (as in the balloons you see at a birthday parties). Balloons were more than just a decoration, which is how the support worker in the house he lived in viewed them; they were so important to him that they had become fundamental to his sense of happiness. She went on to explain how, in agreeing the support plan with Peter and his support workers, she made the balloons central to everything as a best interest decision and advocated strongly for balloons to be central to Peter's support plan which was proceeding before the Court of Protection. She became quite animated, describing how she really got into her stride in court, talking about the importance of the balloons and how without them Peter would very much struggle to function. She explained to the court that without this relationship with balloons the restrictions on this person's liberty would be so severe that they would, in her opinion, leave Peter bereft. Peter loved balloons, all be it that they were an inanimate object. His relationship with the balloons was intimate and important to him. The loss of balloons in his life would place Peter at risk of behaving in a manner which would challenge services and the support workers, exposing Peter to a high risk of him being subject to restraint, medication and other restrictions which would further escalate his behaviours.

The social worker explained how she had ensured that others in the multi-disciplinary team recognised the importance of balloons to Peter, as strange as the concept was to them. She recognised that others in the multi-disciplinary team had struggled with the idea of Peter having a relationship of such weight and importance with balloons. Most had in fact spent years trying to divert Peter's attention away from balloons, thinking it would be in his best interest to give them up and focus on what they felt were more age-appropriate pastimes. In her opinion, however, whilst Peter had a good life and was healthy, clearly he was happier because balloons were in his life. Yes, his life may be enhanced by having a partner, children, increased social opportunities, and all that was for the social worker to continue working on with Peter. But for now Peter, who was subject to being deprived of his liberty, was intimately attached to balloons.

The judge listened to the evidence provided by the social worker and nodded throughout her testimony. At the end the judge said to the social worker, 'If Peter's world is, as you say, so wrapped up in the world of balloons, why then is there no mention of balloons by the Section 12 approved doctor and the Expert Witness, who is a psychiatrist?' The social worker said, 'Because they are both experts on Peter's health condition. However, my observation is that they have never taken the opportunity to get to know Peter as a person. If you know Peter, you know his world revolves around balloons.' The judge smiled and said, 'Quite.'

In our experience we have found it common for social workers to significantly struggle to articulate what they do. In the example of Peter and the balloons how do you wrap that up in a competency or a task or a function of a role? Understanding the relationship between an adult man and inanimate, colourful party accessories is not something that can necessarily be defined. In terms of our work across health and social care understanding the issue of Peter and the balloons and using that to help secure his happiness and minimise state intervention in his life does not neatly sit near a health care procedure, an assessment form or a three-conversation model. The ability to think critically at an advanced level is the key skill here. The social worker was able to explore Peter's relationship with balloons in such a way that she could then passionately and effectively advocate on his behalf. Being able to convey how central the balloons were to Peter's wellbeing illustrates the beauty of social work when we get it right. It is about understanding and being able to articulate the uniqueness of people and their relationships. So, what about when the discussion becomes more intimate, when we bring sex into the conversation? Kirsty Liddard, in her book *The Intimate Lives of Disabled People* (2018), explores how disabled people's sexual politics and their intimate, private lives have become marginalised, resulting in asexuality being imposed on disabled people, who are assumed to lack capacity and capability to express sexuality, sensuality and desire. An example can be seen in the 2017 ruling which Mr Justice Hedley handed down on the case of *CH v a Metropolitan Council* (2017), CH being a 38-year-old man with Down's syndrome and an associated learning disability. CH and his wife were married in 2010. They had lived together, enjoying what was described as 'normal conjugal relations', in CH's parent's house. All went well, until CH and his wife decided in 2014 that they wanted to start a family together. They sought medical advice and help about options for fertility treatment. A clinical psychologist became involved with CH, conducting a mental capacity assessment on his mental capacity to be able to consent to sexual relations. The outcome of the assessment was huge for CH; once he had been assessed as lacking the capacity to consent it meant any sexual activity between CH and his wife was a criminal offence under Section 30 of the Sexual Offences Act 2003. The local authority where CH lived wrote to the couple, instructing them to cease all sexual activity, informing his wife, WH, that if she did not comply, she would be committing a crime and subject to a safeguarding investigation. WH moved out of the marital bedroom and into another room, reducing any signs of intimacy or affection so that she did not confuse CH about their continued relationship.

Just imagine for a minute that this was you. Your partner of four years who you love enough to want to start a family with is now living in the same home as you, but on fear of threat from the state that you will be prosecuted if you show any sign of affection, you cut yourself off and make yourself cold and distant so you do not inadvertently encourage them to think you still love them. CH did not understand why WH had moved into another bedroom; as noted by Justice Hedley, the impact on CH was 'not difficult to imagine' (para 7).

Acting as his litigation friend, CH's sister, SH, brought the case before the Court of Protection in 2016. Notwithstanding that CH and WH were in a committed and monogamous relationship, the expert psychiatrist advising the court recommended that in order for CH to understand the health risks should he be exposed to a sexually transmitted disease from his wife as a result of resuming a normal relationship with her, he needed to attend further sexual education classes to be provided by the therapist who was working with CH. However, there was a delay of over 12 months from the court approving the plan proposed by the psychiatrist, and the sexual education classes taking place. As a result, only on 2 May 2017 were CH and WH allowed by the local authority to resume their normal relationship. The case did not, however, end there. The local authority was challenged under Article 8 of the ECHR, the right to a private and family life, in relation to their conduct towards CH. Judge Hedley, in his commentary, noted that no one sought to argue against the challenge that enforced abstinence from sexual relationships was not a breach of Article 8 as the local authority decided not to contest the case. The local authority offered to make an apology to CH for the delay in arranging for the sexual education classes and paid out £10,000 in damages to CH which was determined by the court to be in CH's best interest. For CH and WH, three years of enforced abstinence, confusion, anxiety, distress. Where was the social work?

On the face of it, this case is straightforward. You could argue, as Justice Hedley did, that in order to protect the vulnerable in society, it is perhaps inevitable that cases such as CH's will arise as the price to be paid (para 15). However, from a social work perspective, was this case inevitable? CH and WH had been married since 2010 and enjoyed a normal and full relationship. Why suddenly in 2014, when the couple sought help from health services to start a family, did professionals decide that CH now needed to be subject to formal assessments about the most intimate aspects of his life? Given that CH and WH were in a committed, monogamous relationship, and that he was able on all other aspects to evidence to the satisfaction of the therapist that he was capacious, why did the psychiatrist recommend that CH needed to go through a further period of sexual education before he could resume his relationship with WH? Why did it then take a further 12 months for the sexual education classes to take place? Given how serious the implications were for CH and WH, you have to ask the question, what exactly were professionals safeguarding CH from?

In researching this chapter, we came across a story of how different it could have been for CH had he had access to better social work. A social worker told us about Lizzie, a young woman who had been referred to her as people were concerned that she needed safeguarding from sexual abuse. The referral was alarming, suggesting that Lizzie was being co-opted into a form of modern slavery by the family of a man who she had only just met but was insisting that she marry. On visiting, however, the social worker found that Lizzie understood the risks, could retain and weigh up the options presented to her and was clear in communicating why the relationship mattered to her. Moreover, she was very clear that she had control over when she did and did not agree to consent to sex with her fiancé. The social worker decided to trust Lizzie and asked if she could arrange to meet with Lizzie and her fiancé together to have a conversation about their hopes and wishes for their lives together. Rather than the aggressive and domineering person she had read about in the safeguarding referral, she found Lizzie's boyfriend to be caring and clearly in love with Lizzie. She closed the safeguarding and instead asked the couple what, if any, support they wanted from her to help them set up a good life together. A year later, she attended their wedding.

When it's understood well, the Mental Capacity Act is the most powerful tool in the social work toolbox. Social work has a unique role, which is defined by a combination of legal literacy, understanding of advocacy and the ability to critically reflect on values in action, to maintain the centrality of power and control with the people social workers support. Being person-centred is enshrined in law as our description of the five principles of the MCA outlines:

1. The person has the right for it to be assumed that they should be in control of whether they want support at all, and if they do how their support is arranged.

2. All practicable steps must be taken to make the decision, including reasonable adjustment to enable them to communicate how they want their support arranging.

3. If they want to arrange their support in a way that doesn't fit the views of professionals – the social workers job is to advocate for them and use the law to enable them to take risks, challenging where professionals and others argue that the risk is unwise and therefore questions the original assumption that the person has the capacity to be in control of how their support is arranged.

4. Any decision taken on behalf of a person who does lack the capacity to make the specific decision must be taken in their best interest. Section 5 of the Mental Capacity Act provides for a defence against liability if the statutory principles are applied. The bar is much lower than most professionals realise when it comes to capacity. The latest analysis shows a 95 per cent increase in the number of requests for the Deprivation of Liberty Safeguards not granted. This includes people who have died since the request was made, but it also includes people who the multi-disciplinary team deemed lacked capacity to be involved in the decision whether to go home or whether to move to a care home, who have subsequently been found to have had the capacity to understand, retain, weigh up and communicate their view once a social worker trained to a higher standard of legal literacy as a Best Interest Assessor has met the person.

5. Any decision taken must be the least restrictive. Rarely will 24-hour settings, such as a care home, a supported living house or a hospital be the least restrictive.

Conclusion

In this chapter we explored how social work practice which recognises love, intimacy and private, personal lives could be central to promoting wellbeing. Intimate social work potentially provides for a fuller, more accurate, account of the person and their circumstances for social workers. Intimate and private lives cannot be explored in a single visit, especially not one where the agenda is pre-determined by a script to be followed as laid out in a large assessment document. For social workers to be able to connect and build trust takes time. Good social work employers recognise that practitioners need to be given permission to build up intimate relationships with people and tackle institutionalised practice which marginalises people's pleasure, sexuality and happiness.

In adult social care, sexual desire is often conflated with concepts of risk and danger. Being able to work positively with professional constructions of risk arising from sex and desire involves a sophisticated understanding and exploration of the notion of risk, seeking to clarify the views of those involved, exploring the ownership of risk and separating out professional anxieties from actual risks. This includes understanding the need for support and interventions that do not to compromise the person's right to a private and personal life through unnecessary and disproportionate state interference and social control. Consider and analyse the role of power in relationships; for example, ask yourself, does this care home allow the person's boyfriend to stay over or do these care staff enable access to sexual aids and accept that masturbation is not restricted to normative notions of 'only on a night' (Liddard 2018)?

Suggested further reading and resources

Neary, M. (2017) *Where Have All the Milkmen Gone?* Self-published, lulu.com

Preston-Shoot, M. and Agass, D. (1990) *Making Sense of Social Work: Psychodynamics, Systems and Practice*. Basingstoke: Palgrave.

Ruch, G., Turney, D. and Ward, A. (2018) *Relationship-Based Social Work: Getting to the Heart of Practice*. London: Jessica Kingsley Publishers.

🐱 You are the social worker: Annabelle

Telephone call from Claire Francis, social worker at Clough Road Resource Centre: 'Annabelle has been extremely difficult to manage today, and staff are tired of having to tolerate her deteriorating behaviours due to reduced staffing levels. Things came to a head yesterday when Annabelle became so difficult at lunchtime that she swore at Sue Connors (Resource Centre Manager) and pushed Sue against a wall as she ran to try and get out of the door, hurting her own hand in the process. Request a safeguarding alert and also agreement for two to one staffing if Annabelle attends the centre again this week.'

Annabelle is a 20-year-old woman with a learning disability. She has been known to social services since birth and she lives with her parents who are both lay preachers at a local Baptist Church.

When you meet with Annabelle, she tells you a 'secret'. She says that she has a boyfriend who is called Imran. Imran is 47 years old and lives alone, having previously been married. Sometimes Imran invites Annabelle to his home and they have a sexual relationship.

Annabelle has told Claire Francis, who is her keyworker at the Resource Centre, who has told Annabelle's parents about Imran. Annabelle has said that her parents have 'grounded' her and have removed her mobile phone to stop her speaking to Imran and have described her behaviour as 'sinful'. Annabelle's parents have also informed the police. Annabelle says the police have visited her at home and told her that due to 'Imran's age compared to hers' they feel the relationship is inappropriate and needs to stop due to the risks.

A social worker responds:

The thing that really stands out for me when I read this case is the utter lack of regard or respect for Annabelle's rights in this situation. She is an adult yet her right to privacy, her right to have a relationship, enshrined in Article 8 of the ECHR, are given no consideration by the professionals involved. This is where the role of the social worker is so important: in upholding and promoting these rights and challenging those that seek to repress and remove them for those they deem to be 'vulnerable'.

As a social worker, taking a rights-based, person-centred approach to working with Annabelle is vital. What are her views, wishes and feelings? How does she feel about her relationship, about going to day care? What are her aspirations, hopes and dreams and how can she be supported to achieve these, if she needs any support at all? The role of the social worker is to keep Annabelle at the centre of all the work they do, working with her and with her consent and not to be distracted or unduly swayed by the concerns and risks expressed by others. In this case this appears to be the age of her boyfriend, the concerns of her parents and the unidentified risks referred to by the police.

If there are genuine reasons to believe Annabelle cannot consent to sexual relationships then a mental capacity assessment can be undertaken with Annabelle, but there is relevant case law including *Sheffield City Council v E* (2004) EWHC 2808 (Fam) and *PH & A local authority v Z limited & R* (2011) EWHC 1704 (COP), which ruled that we must not set test of capacity too high as to do so would run the risk of discriminating against the disabled person in contravention of the Disability Discrimination Act 1995 and Equality Act 2010. The case law is clear: the bar for assessing capacity is low, and any support or education which would enable Annabelle to understand and make the decision must be considered first.

The temptation with situations like this is that as a natural desire for the social worker we want to fix things, and to do so quickly. Clearly Annabelle's human rights have been significantly breached and this should rightly outrage rights-based practitioners. However, the skill of the social work intervention is that the support Annabelle receives is guided entirely by Annabelle. The pace of work, the nature of the relationship to be built between the social worker and Annabelle, and the impact of social workers working on behalf of the state and leaving a profound legacy on the ongoing relationships Annabelle is likely to continue to have (for example with her parents) need to be very carefully considered. An approach that dogmatically upholds Annabelle's rights whilst berating concerned and loving parents, no matter how misguided they may be, is likely to only serve the satisfaction of the social worker in the first instance and could significantly increase further risk to Annabelle. Rights-based social work is rooted in the universally appreciated rights that we all enjoy. A positive relationship with Annabelle's parents, based entirely on the desires and choices of Annabelle and the support of the social worker, is likely to result in further long-term benefits both for Annabelle and also those who love her. It is these relationships in the future, and not social work intervention alone, that will enable Annabelle to experience the freedoms afforded to us all.

Chapter 5

Language, Case Note Recording and Writing about People

IAN BURGESS, ROB MITCHELL, MARK HARVEY and ELAINE JAMES

Introduction

The purpose of this chapter is to encourage social workers to consider how their use of language can impact on their practice and influence the practice of others. It explores some challenging ideas which reference the disability studies literature, which contests that language is a powerfully humanising or 'dis/humanising' tool in the hands of professionals (Goodley 2014; Goodley and Runswick-Cole 2014). The following blog was inspired by language that we have found recorded on far too many assessment forms and support plans, words which many of us as professionals use and have used. You will find some of them in guidance from respected health and social care bodies. For example, 'service user' is a very common term most people reading this will have used at some point. Is it bad? Not necessarily. But why use the term at all? Or any other term which separates 'them' from 'us'?

The blog is called 'No Further Action'. This is reference to the acronym NFA which is found in people's case notes. It is a shorthand for professionals. It is an inadvertently dehumanising act which writes off a person, their whole life, in just three letters.

💬 No further action

IAN BURGESS

When I first qualified as a social worker I had an agency job at a hospital. I got on well with the nurses, I supported the discharge of many older people into care homes and on at least one occasion it was against the woman's wishes. She begged me to get her home, but it was okay because I referred to 'common law' to justify my actions. Her physical needs justified it and everyone (apart from her) agreed, so into a care home she went, the placement processed in less than an hour. I don't know what happened to her next. I do know I was never asked by the home to do any further work about getting her back home. I presume that move was her last one.

I jotted down little medical hieroglyphs on my handwritten notes and used medical jargon on the electronic recording systems. People were 'patients' or sometimes 'service users'. This language protected me from the reality of what I was doing to people caught in the system, lacking power and influence because of their age and disability, unable to square up to professionals like me with our clipboards and our own language.

Social work with adults can be difficult when people are in crisis and experiencing loss, and they pour their pain into you because there is nothing else they can do. And so I learnt that dehumanising people through my use of the language of the professional made it easier for me to cope.

I stopped doing it, very quickly. There was another woman on the ward for whom I was the allocated social worker. I had never met her, but I phoned daily for a progress report. 'How is she?' I asked the nurse.

'Oh, she's very poorly today, not fit for discharge,' said the nurse. On my notes, I wrote, 'TC ward, Pt med', that is, 'Telephone call to the ward, patient medical' (i.e. unwell, not able to be discharged).

Next day the same call, the same note on her records.

The third day I phoned, the nurse told me the woman had died during the night. I wrote 'Pt RIP NFA'; that is, 'Patient dead, no further action'.

I stared at what I had written, and the scales fell from my eyes. If I write about people in this manner, and think of them in this manner, I thought, then what is my treatment of them going to be?

Since then, all my references to people use titles of respect – Mr, Mrs, whatever the person wants. I am not comfortable with the use of initials or 'P' in legal proceedings but the need for confidentiality justifies that, I suppose.

Whatever our opinion about language, dehumanising people is contrary to the ECHR which is grounded in the basic right of every person to be treated with dignity. The Convention rights, incorporated into UK law with the Human Rights Act, were written after the Second World War to prevent the horrors of that period in history from happening again.

I am absolutely not comparing myself or any colleagues in social care to those officials working with the Nazis. But I do believe that we must remain ever vigilant to the use of language which dehumanises people. When we succumb to casual use of dehumanising language, talking up risk in order to impose our will on people, we become party to what Graeber (2015) has called the threat of 'the violence of bureaucracy'. Unchecked, language can take us towards social extremes. 'Us' and 'them'. We are always superior to them. Medics steeped in a professional language with Latin roots feel no such professional angst. Language is a significant symbolic aspect in identifying how medical culture has come to prevail and dominate so-called integrated health and social care despite the espoused 'integrated' nature of multi-disciplinary teams. 'Occupational language' is often used as a means to establish 'superiority' and differentiation (Davies, Nutley and Mannion 2000) through separate codes of professional language. Scott *et al.* (2003) highlight the particular extent to which language in clinical settings, whereby functions and diseases have a standardised Latin nomenclature, is used to 'mystify knowledge' (Meek 1988). Whilst the language of the medic may provide a useful functional framework for a profession, and has its advantage of providing a universal aid to communication regardless of the medic's mother tongue (Scott *et al.* 2003) it also acts a mechanism of conveying dominance (Waitzkin 1989) of one profession and their professional judgement over the other.

I recall the story of the German railway clerk in 1944 who did not consider himself complicit as he wrote in his ledger not of people, but of how many Stücke (literally, 'pieces') he had processed through his station for special treatment that day (i.e. how many people crammed into cattle trucks without water or sanitation he arranged to be transported to a concentration camp). In *A Holocaust Reader* (1976) Lucy S. Dawidowicz refers to bureaucratic language as 'a language that concealed more than it communicated, its very structure and vocabulary buffering speaker and listener from reality' (p.14).

This may feel, and hopefully is, a thousand times removed from our use of language in health and social care. However, if a person is described in terms of being a thing ('a Down's', 'a service user', 'a bed number') rather than a person, is it easier for us to cope with the emotional and physical pain the person is going through and possibly our failure to be able to do anything about it? Does it enable us to sleep at night like the railway clerk? I failed to listen to the woman begging me to let her go home who I processed into a care home; I saw her as a collection of things that had gone wrong and needing to be put right, and discharge to a care home was my solution.

How we think about people and refer to them can become manifest in our practice. I once saw someone working in a care home use a cloth to wipe down a table after lunch and then – without a word or any eye contact with this person – she used the same cloth to wipe the face of a woman still sat at the table who had just finished her lunch and had some food on her chin! That worker could only do that if she did not consider the woman to be equal to her, to be a fellow human being. And how many steps is it from treating a person like that, to neglecting her personal care needs, to hitting her, to stealing from her? Because she is no longer a human, she is a thing. But the care worker would probably never have thought of herself as doing anything mean or bad or hurtful.

As a social worker, I am privileged that the state trusts me to do the job I do. Anti-oppressive practice is central to good social work practice but just because we have a professional qualification, it doesn't mean that we are immune. Far from it; the need to continually critically reflect on our practice and be open to the observations of others, in particular those 'others' who we claim to serve, is an essential part of the job.

The language we use is important because it can very easily be used as a tool to dehumanise people and yet it is also easy to fix. Looking at what we write about people and asking: 'Would I be happy to read this if written by another social worker about me or one of my relatives?' is a good place to start.

The assessment

A social worker recalls chairing a meeting about a man who the local authority had recently placed in a care home. During the meeting he noticed that the man's mother, Sheila, was becoming increasingly frustrated by the meeting; in particular, she became increasingly fidgety as the social worker insisted that he go carefully and line by line through (what was then) a community care assessment. The social worker patiently explained to Sheila that he had to make sure he had captured all the information appropriately and accurately and so that everyone's views were incorporated. Sheila stopped the meeting and said, 'Can I tell you something? I work for a bank and I've studied commerce. You know mini banks? Cash machines? When you put your card in and you want to withdraw cash, what happens? Take me through that process.' Uncomfortable silence ensued. No one spoke; everyone looked down, not wanting to make eye contact with her. After a few moments of awkward silence, she continued. 'Okay. I'll tell you. You type your PIN in and then you issue your instructions to the machine. It asks you if you want information about your balance, receipt and then finally you get cash options. You choose what amount of cash you want. But the crucial thing is that the machine doesn't give you cash straight away. First it gives you back your card and then and only then it gives you your cash. That's deliberate. Does anyone know why?' Again, nothing from the stunned multi-disciplinary team. 'It's because you'll forget your bank card once you see the money because that's what you came for. You will take the money from the machine and turn and walk away and you've forgotten about the process because it's not important. The card will then come out of the machine and the machine will bleep loudly to remind you to take it. If it didn't you would be down the road counting your money and planning on what you're going to do with it. We have research in commerce that evidences that this happens on 90 per cent of transactions we have tested. The product is always the thing, not the process. Your assessment is a process, but it doesn't mean a thing to my son or me. We want action.'

Sheila went on to explain that the 'action' for her son was the care; that was the outcome. The process (the assessment), as she saw it, was for the social worker, not for her and absolutely not something for her son. Social work education can be a moment for reflection and challenge, but it can also be an exercise in training, schooling on the process of transacting the assessment to keep the industrialised processing of people moving through the system. In a typical week, you might find yourself being praised for being a quick worker, one who can be relied on to get six cases completed and progressed through to the funding panel for the health and social care negotiation to commence over who pays for the placement in the care home. We do not dispute that such an approach involves exceptional levels of hard work. It is no easy task to complete a large assessment document. Although over time, there are stock phrases which the most efficient of professionals may find themselves replicating again, and again, and again... And once the assessment is completed, you might visit the care home to see the person again in six weeks to see if they had 'settled in', which is essentially social care code for 'have they given up resisting and are now accepting they are never going home?' Again, this visit will lead to further documentation for the professional to coordinate, complete and submit. The industry of care will keep the most effective care manager busy.

But if the idea of the busy care manager doesn't fit with your view of the type of practitioner you want to be, then perhaps these questions might be ones that you have churning in your mind:

- Who cares about the consequences for the person?

- Once completed, are the assessments I complete ever read again? What happens to them?

- Does anyone other than me read the carefully researched, person-centred pen picture I write in my best assessments?

- In guiding the person through a process of assessment support plan and review am I really being person centred? Is the person really central to decision making?

- Do any of my assessments lead to the people I support being better off?

Your assessments are usually produced after a huge amount of input and work on your part, but really, most assessments consistently result in a small number of very simple to arrange outcomes – home care, respite, day care or residential placement. If the care home says yes, they'll take them, you can forward on the care plan and have the person you assessed settled in ready for the evening meal round. Ultimately the success of the assessment is determined by the availability and accessibility of a set of pre-determined services, which have been commissioned on behalf of the social worker in isolation from the process of capturing and establishing the presenting need for social care. The long-term happiness of the person can be entirely dependent on the quality of these individual providers, your assessment relegated to a static recording of their perspective at a specific point in time which fades into the past as it is superseded by a plethora of new documents to process – support plans, medication charts, meal charts, visitor logs.

Good social work relies not on an assessment form, a care managed process, but rather is genuinely informed by eligibility, by need and by person-centred support that places the person and their opinions as central. The skill of the social worker is in recognising the value of a cuppa and a chat, a frown or a joke, the mention of a relationship, a loving glance between family members. Social work practice shines when social workers recognise that people are the experts of their own lives and experiences.

Sheila and her son were the experts of their lives. The social worker was there to understand environmental and sociological issues and place those in a context of their human rights. That's our role. Let's stop wasting time spending days in the office typing up pages and pages of assessment forms and case notes which no one will read. We are the PIN number, the bleep in the machine, the questions about balance on screen and whether receipts are wanted. We are the action, not the assessment.

Take care with the language you use when writing about people. Think carefully, why I am writing this? What is it going to be used for? How will others read the words I've written and what story will it tell them about the person they are reading about? Take steps to address inequality in your writing. Continuous positive regard is integral to all interactions. Seek to redefine negative views and stereotypes, challenging societal norms that disable the people you work with. Listen to family members, and learn to value their experience and expertise in supporting the person, but do not lose focus on being there for the person. Make use of all the resources available to you to make reasonable adjustments and take all practicable steps to enable and support people to express their wishes, feelings and beliefs. Ultimately, remember that an assessment is just your opinion at a given point in time. It is not an action to make things better for the person or their family. What's the point of writing a huge assessment if it doesn't lead to action which makes for the person experiencing a better life?

Avoiding myths

Mark Harvey reflects on how one morning in the usual rush and chaos to get his youngest son to school, his eldest out of bed and to college, as well as managing to get to work on time, a conversation developed which made him think about what difference social workers make, and how do they know? As he drove both his boys to school/college they asked what he was doing that day. Hearing that he was planning to give a presentation on social work, they wanted to know more: what was he presenting on and why? Mark was presenting that day to the local Partnership Board of self-advocates with learning disabilities about themes of active citizenship and personalisation of support arranged by social workers in his local authority. He recalls how this triggered an in-depth chat, first about the fact that this board had people with learning disabilities as full members and then about what people with learning disabilities can and cannot do and how it must feel if the only people in your life are paid to be there. The conversation soon moved on to discussing the perceived myths around disabled people and why society allows these myths to permeate. As he got out of the car, Mark's son left him with this: 'Well, you're a social worker, isn't it your job to stop these myths? I cannot do it all on my own at college Dad.' He left Mark thinking about how these myths make their way into social work, how without constant self-checking through reflective supervision it can be so easy to start documenting in our assessments, our reviews and our case notes myths which we represent as factual truths about people to justify our actions as professionals.

The top myths which Mark and his son identified were as follows:

1. Disabled people do not have a health condition that requires them to sleep more than everyone else. Therefore, they do not need to get ready for and into bed before the credits on the evening soap have even finished. As social workers we regularly hear that people go to bed early on a night, not due to having had a busy and exhausting day but because that's the way the home they live in operates.

2. Contrary to popular belief, loads and loads of voluntary work doesn't make disabled people 'work ready'. It just means they are contributing back to society like anyone else who volunteers. The hint here is that when people without work want a job, they should be supported to get a job: one that pays them properly and is as interesting and motivating as you would want for yourself.

3. Disabled people do not increase wear and tear to rented properties, requiring landlords to endure a higher risk and financial burden which requires them to be charged a higher, enhanced rate for their rent. It is difficult for a disabled person to be able to become independent if they face high rents which are inflated due to imagined additional costs on the part of the landlord. These prevent them from being able to save up a deposit to move on into their own property or secure a level of income through employment which enables them to take over the tenancy and manage the property themselves.

4. De-registering a residential care home and calling it 'supported living' does not stop it being a residential unit. Group homes, which are organised around the staffing routines of the provider, with no private living, kitchen or bathroom space will always be residential settings regardless of their classification with regulators. This is particularly so

in settings where there are staff on site 24/7 and where the standard model of support is a minimum of one-to-one or even more restrictive.

5. Disabled people are capable of owning and caring for pets. In fact, many do so and gain immense pleasure from the love they share with their pet. People do not need to attend a day centre to pat or stroke a dog, or to go on an organised trip to hold a rabbit, or to have sheep brought into their home to experience lambing season in the spring.

6. Disabled people do not like music any more or less than anyone else. And they do not always need 'special places' to listen and dance. They absolutely do not want to go home to bed at 9 p.m., especially not if the reason they are going home early from the club/gig is because they have medicines they are supposed to take. To quote Paul Richards from the Stay Up Late Campaign, 'How big are the tablets that they can't be taken out with you?' I learnt this from a poster outside a nightclub in Bournemouth which will forever be burnt into my mind. It read: 'Fuck the Gateway Disco, this is a real club where we dance, drink, possibly snog if we're lucky and look out for each other.'

7. Disabled people get angry like everyone else does, but remember when they get angry and have a row with you whilst buttering the toast it does not mean you have a right to record it as 'x was verbally aggressive and brandishing a knife'. It probably means 'I want to eat my toast so no, I'm not getting on the bus right now.'

8. Supported living does not mean you have finally made the step to enabling someone to live a fully independent life, integrated into an inclusive community. This is especially the case when the people who are living in the house did not choose to live together and would not choose to continue to live together if another option was made available.

9. Disabled people do not need longer than non-disabled people to recover from periods of mental ill health. People with learning difficulties and/or physical or sensory conditions

are not automatically 'treatment resistant' if they do not immediately agree with your treatment plan. Years in psychiatric hospitals do not make people super psychiatrically healthy; it just means we are likely to prove our own false hypothesis and keep them admitted longer. Stop over-medicating people with learning disabilities.

Disability is a protected characteristic under the Equalities Act and grounds for reasonable adjustment to everyday life to enable access. Perhaps people with disabilities are just people who have a right to have the world adapted to enable them to participate fully within it as equal citizens.

As observed by Hedley J in *A NHS Trust v P & Anor* [2013] EWHC 50 (COP) the purpose of the Mental Capacity Act is not to provide *'forensic cotton wool'* but to enable individuals to make the *'same mistakes'* as any other human being.

> The plain fact is that anyone who has sat in the Family jurisdiction for as long as I have, spends the greater part of their life dealing with the consequences of unwise decisions made in personal relationships. The intention of the Act is not to dress an incapacitous person in forensic cotton wool but to allow them as far as possible to make the same mistakes that all other human beings are at liberty to make and not infrequently do so.

Conclusion

In this chapter we have argued that good social workers are like chameleons. They blend in. You do not often see them. It's enough for people who need social work to know they're there and that's enough recognition for the social worker too. Social work is not about looking down a deep hole at someone, turning on a blue light and inviting the paparazzi around to film as the drama unfolds. Social workers are not a form of superhero. Better social work practice is about getting into the hole with the person to give them the leg up, so they can wherever possible scramble out of it clinging onto whatever dignity remains. If the person tells someone of the good work of the social worker, then that's great; if they do not, then that's great too. It doesn't lessen what the social worker did. Social workers have their moments of fame. They know their worth. The new creative social work movement is about reimagining a professional identity and model of practice which reflects and enshrines social work values. Social workers are here to enable people to experience the full embodiment of equal human rights as citizens. What's not to love about that?

Our interpretation of critically reflective, rights-based social work practice with adults is more than a simplistic repositioning of ideas of risk management, through reframing risk as sitting firmly with the individual as part of their rights and responsibilities. There are systemic implications for social work recruitment, education and post-qualifying support which we are suggesting. Creativity in social work leadership practice is needed if creativity is to be nurtured and flourish at all levels of practice. The reimagining of the reflective practitioner, working in partnership with people to co-create the future they would want for themselves, needs to know and believe that practice leadership is bought into this approach to practice. The values inherent within relational, ethical professional social work practice are being questioned by increasingly visible and active self-advocacy movements, which are supported by the ease of access to open inexpensive social media distribution channels. The courts are ruling on adult case law in volumes which are unprecedented. Each case ruling before the courts brings a further refinement of thinking about the nuances within human rights law, including the Mental Health Act 1983 and the Mental Capacity Act 2005, with significant implications for the profession

Emerging new technologies are reshaping the professional practice space within which social work identity is influenced and shaped. By amplifying particular voices and messages, social media platforms open up access to diverse networks which front-line practitioners can connect into. Social media presents social work practice leaders with a huge opportunity to reimagine how practice leadership can and should operate. Social media platforms are truly global in nature and could be used to practise leadership as a powerful tool to facilitate exchange of tacit and explicit knowledge about the nature of practice (Rautenbach and Black-Hughes 2012).

Given that social work decision making is multi-dimensional, and defined by inherent power asymmetries, new media provide the opportunity to redress and rebalance, incorporating critically reflective voices of parents, families, carers and others who have experience of the impact of practice (James *et al.* 2017).

There are lots of factors which influence how professional social workers define themselves. If the shackles of care management are truly being rejected by the profession, social workers will need to be supported to test their own boundaries and levels of professional risk that they carry. Social work leadership will need to provide clarity over the level of professional autonomy, access to resources and CPD, the professional relationships between agencies in the sphere of practice that social workers operate. Most importantly, social work practice leadership will need to be explicit in describing how social work values fit with, or otherwise, those of the agencies that become the employing organisation of social workers. If social workers embrace the idea of social work being the safeguard of people's human rights, then they will need social work employers to be able to similarly adapt and integrate the new paradigm to prevent social workers finding themselves in an invidious position.

Social workers choose to enter the profession for a reason, they are employed as social workers for a reason and good social workers choose never to forget those reasons. The biggest risk to social work is social work itself: practitioner apathy to personal reflection, development and growth and the 'rust-out' we described in Chapter 1. However you choose to reflect on your own practice, remember that good social workers always need to challenge themselves before they can challenge or support others. Good social workers trust in people and hold a belief that humanity in all its forms is a cause for celebration regardless of the personal challenges people face. To be in social work is to be surrounded by wonder and hope and opportunity.

Suggested further reading and resources

Beresford, P., Fleming, J., Glynn, M. and Bewley, C. (2011) *Supporting People: Towards a Person-Centred Approach.* Bristol: The Policy Press.

Dawidowicz, L. (1976) *A Holocaust Reader.* Library of Jewish Studies. West Orange, NJ: Behrman House Inc.

Stay up Late Campaign: https://stayuplate.org/

You are the social worker: John

Telephone call from Forest View Residential Care Home at 2.30pm on a Friday afternoon: 'John has gone AWOL, he's off his meds and we're really worried about him.'

John moved to the residential care home following a stay in a mental health hospital, when he was 17. He is now 23. John has a diagnosis of autism and a mild learning disability. John's parents are separated. The care home report that he regularly absconds and goes missing. He is on medication to control his behaviours as he is regarded as a risk to himself and others. John is subject to the DoLS, which have been authorised by the Court of Protection to require him to live at the care home.

When you visit the care home you check the incident logs. You note that John usually absconds on a Friday and returns on the following Monday. He is usually found at his brother's house, his brother being two years older than him. There are various multi-disciplinary team assessments associated with John's record which describe concerns about his sexual behaviours. The incidents cover the period of time when he was aged 9 to 14. No concern was substantiated through a safeguarding inquiry, and the police chose not to pursue any action. There are no further documented incidents in the last nine years. Case notes record that John's mum wants him to come home to live with her, but she also states that she cannot cope supporting him on her own.

A social worker responds:

There is a clear discrepancy between the court-approved plan and John's wishes, evidenced by John's regular weekend visits to his brother. One issue with any court is that it can only make a decision based on the evidence placed in front of it. In John's case it is unclear as to whether the court has heard of his frequent stays with his brother or indeed the fact that his mother would like him to return home. Remember, just because there is an order in place doesn't mean that circumstances haven't changed. John may well now (if he ever didn't) have capacity, and such changes in circumstances need to be taken back to the court for a more informed decision.

First, John is currently safely with his brother and there is clear evidence from previous experiences he will return on Monday. Is John then 'AWOL'? No, he has gone to see a family member over the weekend, most probably to either gain a sense of normality or have a break from what has become normality (who doesn't do that on a weekend?). So, advise the home to leave John where he is. Then the real social work starts.

Meet John, build up a relationship with John and get to know why John goes to see his brother. Is John happy with his current arrangements? Is he aware his mum would be happy to have him back home with some support? John is 23 he has a whole life ahead of him. Where does he see himself in five, ten, fifty years' time? Justice Jackson, when hearing Steven Neary's case (2011) proposed that Article 8 ECHR, the right to private and family life, is the nub of the matter when determining what is in a person's best interest; in John's situation this is exactly the case. Where does John call home? Why isn't he there? Uphold John's Article 8 rights if he wants to live with his mother, with his brother or remain where he is; take this to the court.

John is also being viewed and portrayed as a sexual offender. It appears that when John was a child he had some periods of experimenting with others. However, there are no offences or conditions imposed on John currently. This would indicate these sexual behaviours may not have been as serious as the multi-disciplinary team are suggesting. Coupled with the fact that no such issues have arisen in over nine years, I think it would be safe to say the matter of inappropriate sexual behaviours is not an issue. As professionals we tend to talk up risk or professionalise normality, such as normal sexual development, as 'sexual behaviours'. This then provides the necessary justification for intervention in people's lives.

Within this I think we lose sight of who we work for; we become the professional, the expert. John pays our wages, he pays your manager's wage and your manager's manager's wage. Treat him with the same respect and dignity you would your own boss, because he is!

Chapter 6

Safeguarding

ROB MITCHELL and ELAINE JAMES

Introduction

'Find me somebody to love', a lyric from the band Queen. A lyric which has endured over 40 years. It conveys the aching, human desire for connection with another human. To love and be loved. There can be nothing greater. 'Someone to safeguard' was originally written as a reflective piece about social work we have been involved with where we made the person's life worse. Our involvement focused on our own power, and not on listening to what Elsie really needed and not hearing and respecting what she was telling us about what was important to her. The blog about our experience supporting (or failing to support) Elsie has been our most successful ever and continues to be so, with around a hundred new people every month finding it. 'Someone to safeguard' asks us to consider what the cost is to the person when we allow the protection imperative to take hold of us. As professionals we have the power to displace people's autonomy and impose a host of restrictions on their freedom. We have to be continually alert to this risk. The trick to being powerful is to know how and when to exercise that power and when to exercise restraint.

Someone to safeguard

ROB MITCHELL

The referral was pretty bog standard these days. The neighbours didn't get Elsie's permission for any of her details to be referred to social services. In truth, it had never crossed their minds they'd be asked for this. When pushed by the call centre about the issue of consent they said that they didn't think they needed her consent and that this was a matter that 'the Council must take seriously for everyone's sake'. And then behind the thinly veiled threat to act, the neighbour stumbled upon four little words. Magic words. Words that suddenly change the meaning of everything and words that seemingly come with their own legislation, procedures, judges and juries. 'It's a safeguarding issue.' And boom, there it is. Elsie, aged 87, never having failed to pay for council services or any other tax that funded the welfare state she chose not to use, was known. Consent overridden. Case opened. Within moments Elsie had an electronic file. Elsie had a reference number. And Elsie would receive an automated letter thanking her for contacting the Council and she would receive a call within the next seven days. All done within five short minutes from the start of the phone conversation. Within ten minutes Elsie was on a waiting list of other reference numbers waiting to be allocated to a social worker and sitting on the computer screen of the manager. Whether Elsie used services or not, from that moment on to the day of her death, nothing was clearer – Elsie was now a service user and there was a record to prove it. There was, as far as everyone was concerned, someone to safeguard.

The social workers went in twos to the address. No one was quite sure why. The referral mentioned that Elsie had got cats but there was not any belief that the cats were dangerous. Perhaps the second social worker was there because social workers love cats. The referral said the house was 'dirty', 'things everywhere', 'cluttered', 'soiled pads in the garden' and Elsie, although not seen for some weeks, was wholeheartedly felt by the neighbours to be dirty herself. 'She's self-neglecting.'

Having knocked at the door and got no response, the social workers pushed slightly at it and the door opened. A cat ran out and then back in again. No sign of Elsie in the hallway. The social workers called her name, walking gingerly through the hallway, past a sideboard with some framed pictures of a moustachioed man with 'Geraldo, King of Swing' emblazoned on them. Calling out her name and holding out their ID badges the social workers continued inward.

Elsie was in the kitchen. She smiled when she saw the social workers and beckoned them in still further. The social workers introduced themselves and whilst doing so Elsie kept on smiling before raising her hand as if to stop the second social worker saying their name. Elsie bent forward and placed her right ear up against what looked like an old radio from footage used to show listening to the broadcasts of Prime Minster Churchill telling them they wouldn't surrender to the Nazis. Almost trance like Elsie's smile remained fixed as she listened to the radio. Elsie probably listened to the radio for a full three minutes; to the social workers, observing the cats, the newspapers (one from May 1991 with a picture of Paul Gascoigne on it) and moving their feet on the sticky floor tiles, the three minutes felt like a lifetime.

When Elsie moved away from the radio, she asked the social workers, 'Who are you again, love?' The social workers explained who they were and said that they were there to see if 'she was alright, you know, see how things are'. Elsie said she was fine and asked if the neighbour had asked for them to visit. 'She's lovely, like that. Looks out for me.' Elsie explained that she had lived in the house all her life. Her parents, who she told the social workers 'died recently, in 1971 and 1975', had left the house to her. The social workers listened. They wanted to be respectful, they had questions of course (and they had lots of boxes to tick) and had already decided that things 'weren't right' but they listened nevertheless. Halfway through talking Elsie's eyes suddenly lit up. 'John!' she said. Within moments Elsie was back to the other side of the kitchen, head propped up against the radio, same expression on her face, which now to the social workers seemed almost rapturous. This time a longer wait. Five minutes. Elsie broke her concentration just once, to beckon the social workers to sit down. Neither did. Elsie didn't notice or care.

Elsie said that John worked for the radio. He was in his late 40s and his job was a 'broadcaster' and that each day John 'either announced the news or introduced big bands...sometimes both'. Elsie said that John was based in London and he still lived there. She said John sometimes slept in the radio station and sometimes broadcast during the night, but not usually. The social workers continued to listen but really wanted to talk about the cats and

Elsie's 'daily routine and keeping clean'. More in an effort to wrap the conversation up about John and move on to the matter at hand, the self-neglect, one of the social workers asked a question. 'John sounds lovely. Is he someone you have actually met and know?' And with that the tone of the conversation changed. Elsie explained that John had spoken to her on the radio for over 60 years. He was her man friend and he was engaged to marry her. Her betrothed. John had promised Elsie that one day he would drive up from London in a white Bentley car and marry her. Their plan was to live in London and take Elsie away from all this, including the cats. Elsie said the social workers could have the cats if they wanted them.

On walking to the door with the social workers Elsie thanked them for coming but they had to go now as John liked to 'talk to her alone'. Elsie smiled as she shut the door behind them. The last thing the social workers heard Elsie say as the door closed was that John was her man and 'was not for sharing, goodbye'.

The social workers weren't inexperienced. One had just become an AMHP and the other had worked with older people for years. But as they walked to their car and drove back to the office the silence between them spoke more than any words of completed boxes on the safeguarding form. 'What was all that about?'

Safeguarding referrals can be complex. The social workers knew that. They also knew that to 'help' Elsie they had to get to know her, build up trust, etc. So, the visits continued throughout the next week. On no occasion did it occur to the social workers to contact and arrange for an advocate to be there. Elsie was on her own. They were the professionals. They would be able to work out how to protect her. On each occasion Elsie spoke to the social workers but continued to ignore any questions about her health, her wellbeing, her cats and the state of her house. Most questions were met with 'I know love. John will see to it.' All conversations were interspersed with long periods of Elsie listening to the radio and smiling with occasional, knowing nods and some 'yes love' aimed at the social workers as if 'John' was further confirming plans that would need to be relayed to the social workers. For the most part, the social workers just heard the hiss of the untuned radio. For them there was no voice, no programme and without doubt there was no John. However, what bothered the social workers more than this was that there was no progress. No getting Elsie to see what state she was in. No getting Elsie to consent to sorting the house. No getting Elsie to realise the safeguarding issue. The self-neglect. The abuse.

Safeguarding doesn't allow for stalemate or for someone to continue to be abused. It identifies the abuse and through a list of 'outcomes' it makes the social workers do something. For the social workers things needed fixing for Elsie. She had a choice. Either Elsie worked with them to 'improve the situation' or they would 'refer to other agencies'. The case notes were clear. Elsie wouldn't engage. She lacked capacity to make the decision. It was all in her best interests. The risks were unmanageable. The hoarding was a fire risk. The cats were underfed and the RSPCA would be cross. She needed safeguarding. If only she could see it! She was a problem. The problem needed fixing.

The social workers didn't seek Elsie's consent to refer to other professional agencies. In Elsie's case, the 'other agencies' was the Community Mental Health Team. Elsie was visited by a community psychiatric nurse, who within hours visited again but this time with the psychiatrist. The social workers received a call: 'How has this gone on so long?' and 'she's in a terrible way, totally delusional, paranoid ideation' and is 'refusing all treatment because of this bloody John thing.' The next call was to the AMHP. Pink papers in the bag, the Mental Health Act assessment was to take place that evening. No one thought to ring for an Independent Mental Health Advocate.

The ambulance couldn't stay and eventually the police were called. Eighty-seven-year-old Elsie was escorted out of her property by two young police officers. One of the police officers had to switch the radio off during 'the incident' in the house. He at least had the foresight to give the radio to Elsie and reassured her that she 'could hold it' in the back of the car. It was the only bit of humanity Elsie ever witnessed either that evening or throughout her entire dealings with the 'support' agencies. Section 2 completed. Safeguarding outcome achieved. No more self-neglect. Someone had been safeguarded.

The first thing Elsie did on the ward was to find a plug for the radio. John was there. Reassuring her and helping her to stop crying. And that's how things stayed for a number of weeks. The medication was taken, Elsie complied. The nurses moved on to the next person, Elsie listened to John. There were no more worries being reported about Elsie from the neighbours; the problem had been fixed. No more self-neglect; no more self to neglect. Elsie's care plan said 'needs all cares'. And that's what she had. All cares attended to and a continued love affair with John.

The discharge planning never once considered home. Home was where the 'multi-disciplinary team' had felt that the bad thing happened. Home was where the cats had had to be removed and where the social workers had found Elsie's love letters to John, which had ensured merriment on the ward due to the details that she went into about her feelings for him. The self-neglect would re-start at home and why risk things? Elsie was happy enough. Everything was fixed, apart from the John thing.

The care home never fully read the care plan about Elsie and the new social worker had not really written much up about John and what had happened at home. The radio didn't go with Elsie to the care home. Elsie noticed this on her first day at the home. However instead of asking for the radio Elsie screamed for eight hours. In the end she was given medication. The care home didn't call the hospital or speak to the psychiatrist about how distressed Elsie was. They made one phone call that day, which was to the social worker requesting more funding 'due to the screaming' and the impact this was having on other patients and staff.

Over the next three months Elsie moved into two different care homes and was returned to hospital following a fall. The radio was never switched back on.

Elsie died in a care home. It was four months, five days and six hours after the phone call from the neighbour.

Adult protection?

P was a 91-year-old retired civil servant, who had served as an RAF gunner during the war. He lived alone in his own house with his cat Fluffy until he was forcibly removed to a dementia specialist care home by social workers who were responding to an adult safeguarding concern. In the case of *Essex County*

Council v RF & Ors, which became known as 'Fluffy the Cat', District Judge Mort ruled that:

> It is hard to imagine a more depressing and inexcusable state of affairs. A defenceless 91-year-old gentleman in the final years of his life was removed from his home of 50 years and detained in a locked dementia unit against his wishes. Had it not been for the alarm raised by his friend RF he may have been condemned to remain there for the remainder of his days. There can be no doubt that ECC's practice was substandard. They failed to recognise the weakness of their own case and the strength of the case against them. They appeared unprepared to countenance any view contrary to their own. They maintained their resolute opposition to P returning to his home until the last possible moment. In my judgment the conduct of ECC has been reprehensible. The very sad and disturbing consequences for P cannot be ignored.

In the main, people working in social care choose to do so because they want to be caring. But sometimes they do not support people to live the lives they want to lead. Perhaps it's the surprisingly ordinary, possibly even dull nature of an ordinary life which leads to workers talking up worries. This can lead to a reframing of the ordinary act of asking another person for advice or help being turned around and becoming a problem to worry about, evidence of a dependency, a vulnerability the person needs protecting from. Under intense pressure, good people can behave badly and poor organisational culture, usually hidden, can be exposed. In the midst of heightened anxiety, consideration of human rights, issues of consent and evidence of compassion can be the first things to go. Issues of choice and control, foremost in social work values, are at risk of being overridden and drowned out, replaced by the dehumanising language of the day: 'patient', 'green cross', 'system block', 'the admission', anything but people like Elsie being known by their name. Massive pressure can be transferred onto social workers, to shunt poorly people in need of care, compassion, support and access to therapy and nursing into care homes without any consideration of their capacity to be involved in decisions about how their care needs are met or their right to advocacy. As the case of *London Borough of Hillingdon v Neary & Anor* EWHC 1377 (2011) made clear, there is an obligation on you as a social worker to arrange for a suitable person to provide advocacy and safeguard the person's rights where a person lacks the capacity to make the decision about moving into a care home for the purposes of care and treatment (Section 7 DoLS CoP). Steven Neary was detained by social workers for nearly 12 months against his wishes. His father, Mark Neary, took the case to court, successfully arguing that by failing to arrange for advocacy for Steven, he had been denied the right to speedy judicial review of the lawfulness of the detention. Justice Peter Jackson ruled that:

> By keeping Steven Neary away from his home between 5 January 2010 and 23 December 2010, Hillingdon unlawfully breached his right to respect for his family life, contrary to Article 8 ECHR. By keeping Steven Neary at the support unit between 5 January 2010 and 14 April 2010, Hillingdon unlawfully deprived him of his liberty, contrary to Article 5(1) ECHR.

Mark Neary has a deeper insight into the role and purpose of social work than most. He is clear about what he wants when it comes to social work's contribution towards Steven's life. Our impression of Mark, based on his blog and having listened to him speak about his son, is that he doesn't want someone who thinks they know Steven and Mark better than Steven and Mark know themselves. He doesn't want an admin officer for a social worker or someone who can broker care (although he does want the awful bureaucracy removing!). Mark doesn't want someone who can interpret other professionals' jargon on his behalf; he is perfectly able to do that for himself. Mark is not looking for a friend to hang out with for him or Steven. Nor is he looking for someone to relay decisions made by the great and good at panels in locked away towers. Mark wants someone alongside Steven. Someone batting for him. Someone who when Mark is not there is absolutely going to advocate for his son's wishes, feelings, values and beliefs in a way Mark knows Steven wants. Crucially, Mark and others want someone on behalf of the state (local authorities or NHS – it shouldn't matter) who totally get and love the fact that Mark and Steven love each other. The thought of standing in the way of their relationship should be as abhorrent as the feelings generated when you hear Mark talk about those who separated Steven from his dad. Whether it's the principles of the Mental Capacity Act 2005, the Articles in the UNCRPD or the wellbeing principle in the Care Act 2014, the overriding ethos is that the state should not interfere with family life. Our role is to promote it, protect it and if possible, to enhance it... And then get out of the way very quickly! If ever there was a test of social workers' convictions and values, it happens when huge pressure is applied to transfer people into care homes. The decision to move people into care homes must never be taken without consideration of the wishes, feelings and beliefs of the person, and yet it so often is, with heartbreaking consequences.

Rob Mitchell recalls that pressure being applied from his first day in post. Rob remembers how his qualification arrived in the mail just two days before he was due to start that first ever social work post that he had fought so hard for:

New social workers, in the days before we defined newly qualified social workers, were just called new social workers. However, despite the feelings of being welcomed that I had experienced at the interview, the fact that I was newly qualified was never discussed again. From day one – I was a social worker. All the support that had been offered to me as a student and which provided me with a safety net was no longer there. I found myself faced for the first time with the ethical dilemma of being a decision maker.

There are various ways that people adapt in response to the scary moment of realising that you are now making decisions. One is to reject the premise of the question, to realise the arrogance of the assumption that you should be making decisions and to draw on your social work training and values as you remind yourself that your role should be to support the person to remain in control of their life. Another, which I was disappointed to find was the preferred choice of the team I had joined, was to hide behind the protective covers of care management.

I met my first line manager for the second time, in the first hour of the first day; the eyes were as kind as I had remembered from the interview. However, this time she was distracted, clearly really busy, and I was to be fitted into her schedule in between the incessant ringing of the phone and queue of people at her desk. She talked at me a lot, and I sat feeling a mix of confusion, anxiety and boredom as notepad in hand I tried to follow her and make notes. I noticed that she nodded in approval as I wrote down key things that she had said to me. She told me that I was not here to practise social work. I was told I was in fact a care manager. As a care manager, I was told I had a range of solutions for people designed to keep them safe. That's what people knew about social workers. Social workers keep people safe. These solutions became my care management box of tricks. They included a safeguarding assessment and care brokerage. Care brokerage led to one of five things: home care; day care; respite care (which I learnt was code for tricking people into permanent care); residential care; and nursing care. All roads led to care and all care led to a charging assessment. My job was not to challenge; it was to assess social care needs, it was to ensure eligibility and it was to safeguard resources, manage budgets within ever-decreasing expenditure headings and manage people's expectations.

As I tried to absorb this and recover from the jolt to my system, I heard my manager say to me – 'so, I've allocated Jean to you. She's in hospital, she's medically fit and the ward want her gone. She needs an assessment to see what the options are; go and meet her and write down the relevant points so that we can make a decision. The ward are clear, she is a safeguarding and she can't go home'. She handed me a community care assessment form and told me to go and fill it in. I hadn't been prepared for being in at the deep end from day one. But this was what I had trained for, I was a social worker. I loved people, I loved their stories, I could do this.

I met Jean on the ward. She was sat upright in bed with a cup of tea on a table by her side. Jean fascinated me from the moment I met her. Bright eyed and full of mischief, she was starved of conversation in hospital. Presented with the opportunity to talk to someone, anyone who was interested in her and her life story, she was ready to share her life history. Jean told me about her life. And I listened. She had been married for over 30 years when, just shortly after retiring from his job, her husband Bob had died suddenly. She had found herself alone in the house they had raised their children in together. Both had moved on in their lives and away, one as far away as Australia. She desperately missed the phone calls from her grandchildren at 3 a.m. in the morning which had been stopped whilst she was on the ward. And she was very worried about her cat, Sam, who was being looked after by the neighbour whilst she was in hospital. Lost in her memories she told me about how Sam had been a lifeline after Bob had died. One of the ladies at her club had asked Jean if she would be interested in adopting a kitten from a litter they'd had. Unsure at first because she'd never owned a pet before, she'd fallen in love with the tiny black kitten with white socks on his paws and a white patch over his eye the instant she'd met him. From day one, despite her best intentions, she had found herself letting him curl up next to her on the bed and had felt reassured by his presence and comforted by his warmth. She loved Sam. I knew from my social work education that pets are associated with psychological and emotional wellbeing. And so, I listened and made careful notes about how her pet, Sam, was important to Jean.

Back at the office I was determined to show myself in my best light. I had sat with Jean, listening, for over three hours. I had so much material to write up. I wrote pages and pages on the assessment form, staying late that day to get it completed and handed in before I went home. I linked my findings to theory and made sure I had emphasised what really mattered to Jean. I carefully completed a risk assessment to inform a decision about safeguarding concerns raised by the nurses working with Jean. The next morning, I got in early, only to find that my manager had been in earlier still. She asked me to sit with her and talk me through the assessment. Proud of my work, I did so. I then sat back and waited to be told – well done. There was a long pause and then, she passed her verdict – 'You've only gone and assessed the bloody cat.'

I was flummoxed. I felt my world fall into a tailspin. Those kindly eyes looked on with pity as my manager told me about care management. My role was to assess, support, plan using a standard set of solutions from the social care box of tricks – home care, day care, respite, residential care. Sometimes I was to assess jointly with health. This would lead to nursing care. I needed to be quick and get things turned around so that I could move on to the next assessment. Jean was not at risk from others, she was not a safeguarding; Jean needed to be got home with four calls a day from a home care agency and my job was to document this, pick up the phone to the home care agencies and ring until I found one that could start as soon as possible. It didn't matter what the quality of their support was; what mattered was that they could start tomorrow so we could move Jean off the ward and free up the bed.

I didn't manage to see or speak to Jean again. I did as I was told. I set up the home care and moved on to the next referral. It took me a long time to feel confident enough to ask the question – how is this the social work I trained for?

Conclusion

This chapter started with a lyric from the band Queen about finding somebody to love. It goes on to call for relational social work which recognises the need for human beings to have others in their lives who value and love them. In this chapter we have argued that good social work practitioners use critically reflective supervision to incorporate theory, academic literature and continuing professional development to inform and explore wider practice and societal issues, seeking to find alternatives that promote choice, rights, autonomy, partnership and control. They also use supervision to make sure that they never lose sight of the individual person they are supporting, their inherent dignity and humanity. Talking about power, loneliness, hope and hopelessness, and love and happiness are as important to good social work which safeguards adults at risk of abuse as being able to recite multi-agency procedures and protocols. Make sure every week you have time in the office with your colleagues so that you can access support and advice about the lives of the people you are contacting. Plan your diary so that you prioritise your reflective supervision and have time to prepare for it. Investigate post-qualifying awards which will enable you to further develop as a rights-based practitioner, able to draw with confidence on relevant and current case law. Every social worker will experience a circumstance which will define their practice, a case which does not go the way that they had hoped. Critically reflect, learn and be authentic and honest about your feelings when this happens. Most of all be human, be brave, be true to your social work values.

Suggested further reading and resources

Meyerson, D.E. (2001) *Tempered Radicals: How People Use Difference to Inspire Change at Work*. Boston, MA: Harvard Business School Press.
Neary, M. (2010) *Get Steven Home*. lulu.com
Simcock, P. and Castle, R. (2016) *Social Work and Disability*. Cambridge: Polity Press.

🐱 You are the social worker: Mr Smith

Telephone call from the neighbour of Mr Smith: The neighbour reports that Mr Smith is an 88-year-old man who lives alone in the flat opposite her. He is often seen coming and going from his flat but he seems quite a private man. Recently it's been noted that Mr Smith has been calling at his local shop and buying alcohol. When the shopkeeper asked him who the drink was for, he said 'the girls'. There have been some young eastern European women visiting Mr Smith's flat at all hours.

Mr Smith is known to adult social services. He recently received some support via a home care visit to remind him to take his medication. He is known to the Memory Service and has a good relationship with his GP who visits very frequently.

When you visit Mr Smith, he tells you that he is fine and that the alcohol is 'for the girls'. During the discussion he tells you that he thinks that the young women who visit him are sex workers. He says that he likes them to use his flat to keep them warm in the winter. Mr Smith says the women do not pay him for the drink and that he would never dream of asking them as they are his guests. During the discussion Mr Smith tells you that one of the young women (Ursula) is now his girlfriend. You also notice that on the side of the chair when Mr Smith sits there is some unopened medication for the previous few weeks. On the way out of Mr Smith's flat he mentions to you that he has lent his son £500 and he hasn't seen him for a few weeks. Mr Smith asks if you can ring him and remind him to visit his dad and bring the money with him.

A social worker responds:

The first thing is, of course, to speak with Mr Smith. I would do this before speaking with anyone else, though I would check on his records whether there were any communication needs or times which would be best to meet with Mr Smith.

I would be honest and open with Mr Smith about the reasons for my visit. I would tell him that a neighbour has raised a concern. If the neighbour wanted to remain anonymous, that could still be respected, but it would be unacceptable to visit Mr Smith and expect him to answer questions about his private business without explaining why.

If a safeguarding concern has been raised under Section 42 of the Care Act 2014, that still does not remove his right to respect for private and family life; Mr Smith could tell me to mind my own business and, unless there was evidence of risk to others (for example), that could be the end of the matter. Put another way, I would have to consider what would happen if Mr Smith was not an older person but aged 40, or if he was not known to social services. We cannot discriminate and make judgements, no matter how well intentioned, based on age or appearance.

However, given the concerns raised and the factors involved, it would not be unreasonable to at least rule out the possibility that Mr Smith is being coerced or abused in some other way. But still, if he chooses to do what others may consider unwise, that is his business. I would only consider a mental capacity assessment if there was something in his presentation which made me question his ability to make specific decisions, or if someone else was of the opinion that Mr Smith might not be able to make the decision because of mental impairment or if he had previously been determined to lack the mental capacity to make a specific decision.

Mr Smith says he has given his son money, and it appears that this is normal behaviour for him. Perhaps, in other words, he is a generous and kind man of whom people can take advantage, but that could have happened to him at any time in his life. I would put that to Mr Smith and ask if he wanted me or anyone else to do something about it.

I would be happy to ring Mr Smith's son, but I'd ask him if he has tried without success and maybe make the call there and then with

Mr Smith present. If the son was not forthcoming, I would likely take the matter further; for example, speak with the police but again, this would be with Mr Smith's consent.

If Mr Smith has memory problems but can chat openly about 'the girls', I would be inclined to ask about his relationship with them insofar as what they get from the relationship and what he gets from it. Again, this is a very personal matter; I, and most people reading this, do not need to account for my private business to social workers and neither does Mr Smith. I would make that very clear.

The issue of the medication is a cause for concern. I would ask Mr Smith about his medication, ask if I could speak with his GP and ask his GP to determine the risk of not taking medication. Given he has some formal support to take his medication, I would want to know from the provider why he has been missing it (if he has been missing it). I would also be interested to hear what the visiting support staff have to say and would be surprised they had not themselves raised a concern given that they are visiting daily, if it is an issue. There could be any number of reasons for the medication being there; for example, it could be some medication Mr Smith had previously mislaid and only found that morning. I am a social worker, not a detective, and always have regard for the truth that whatever the social work intervention in a person's life, the outcome must be better for the person than what went before. Otherwise there is no point in my being there.

There could be very good reasons for all of this, and my approach must not be affected by any presumptions or prejudices.

If Mr Smith's mental capacity to make the decision to have these women visit his home is in question, then time and decision-specific assessments of capacity may be necessary, but I would equally be mindful of what the outcome might be in the event that Mr Smith could not make the decision(s) because of a mental impairment. Imagine, for example, that the opinion of the neighbour is that the women should be prevented from visiting, even if there is no evidence of crime being committed or, if there is evidence, the chances of a successful prosecution could be very low (considering section 44 of the Mental Capacity Act 2005). How could such restrictions be achieved? Move Mr Smith against his will into care?

Would Mr Smith be happier as a result? Of course, as we have seen from various examples in the Court of Protection (e.g. *SR v A Local Authority* (2018) EWCOP 36) local authorities do not have the authority to simply move people they consider to be at risk into a care setting against their will. They need an order from a court to do that.

Mr Smith's happiness and privacy would be my main motivations in any social work intervention with him; a very respectful and cautious approach would be in order and any intervention would be with Mr Smith's consent, or, if not (because he hadn't the capacity to decide), would be necessary and proportionate with evidence to support that.

But it is not unlikely that Mr Smith is merely enjoying the company of the young women and given that his GP and a domiciliary care provider are regularly calling in and have not reported anything, the concerns as raised by the neighbour may be nobody's business but Mr Smith's.

Chapter 7

The Rise of the New Social Work Bohemians

MARK HARVEY, ELAINE JAMES and HANNAH MORGAN

So, you've read our book. And so, you want to be (or remain) a social worker. Why? That has to be the first question. Not why as in, 'Why on earth would you want to be a social worker?', but why as in, 'if you don't know why, then you had best work it out before you become one'.

Throughout our careers we have been involved in a number of conversations about social work and what it means to be a social worker. Not just as in, what it means to be an English local authority-employed social worker processing care management processes on behalf of an integrated health and social care multi-disciplinary team. But more importantly than that, what it means to be a social worker as a person. Can you separate the role and the person?

Clare Evans, writing in *Community Care* magazine in 2015, asserted that social work training is not taught in a way that is fit for modern practice. Evans suggested that teaching 'social policy and...out dated social worker theories' was no longer helping people and the delivery of social work. The important bit for us in her article, on top of Clare being a disabled woman and working for a user-led organisation, was that she argues for a firm value base and the ability to provide simple practical support. Evans talks about students 'getting it', by which we infer that it's getting the social model and also about being able to critically engage with evidence that matters. There has also been a great deal of debate in the media, amongst politicians and within the profession itself, about the future of social work education. We strongly believe that social work is an intellectual discipline which requires continual engagement with the social model of disability through research in action if it is to continue to be relevant to the people it seeks to serve. Further, we would argue that social work practice has still yet to fully reflexively respond to the extent required to meet the type of reflection in and on action envisaged by Donal Schön (1983). A social work world without a theoretical base for practice took us to the wasteland that dominated since the 1990s community care reforms and places the profession at risk of irrelevance within the current policy context of integration alongside a strong tradition of research and evidence-led health care practice. To reconnect with an idea of social work, the profession must reinvigorate its conception of its purpose as an ethically framed form of social science.

In the same year as Clare's article, George Julian wrote a blog called 'Thoughts on Being Human' (2015) in which she questioned why post-Winterbourne (let alone pre-Winterbourne) and #JusticeForLB there was no tangible voice of social work in the debates about the lives of people with learning disabilities, a profession which makes grand claims about its role in upholding social justice. Julian was provocative, observing 'social work's failure', especially of learning disabled people and their families, to challenge the status quo and drive through an ethical values base which upheld the inherent dignity of all humans as a centralising principle for practice. As social work leaders we must continually reflect on how abuse and neglect took place and continues to take place on our 'social work watch'. Is this the outcome of non-reflective practice, a lack of critical thinking which is being sacrificed so that we blend into integrated health and social care systems where lack of a sufficiently well-developed empirical evidence base for adult social work practice leaves us exposed and vulnerable? Is it a natural conclusion of losing any sense of social work as an identity, lost to care management brokerage that anyone with good relational practice skills could perform?

Is politically aware and engaged social work the norm or is it at risk of becoming the domain of a few institutionalised loud but distant voices? It is with concern that we hear conversations between social workers dismissing the role of politics in social work. One such conversation took place in the run up to the 2017 UK General Election. Sitting in a room with 30 social workers, it became evident that most were uninterested and unaware of the issues let alone intending to vote, a response which felt alarming. Social work if nothing else is innately political, informed by politics, designed by politics, promoted and nurtured or irreparably damaged by politics. Social workers are often agents of the state; they are by nature political and should be politicised. It is not possible to be a good social worker and to be objectively removed from the issues and the political world social workers live and work within. Social workers should be continually interested in and engaged with policies that support or hinder the rights of people in the communities which social work serves, and social workers should not be neutral in response to issues that fundamentally shape the way social workers practise and the lives of the people social workers support.

Too often we have experienced social workers who hide behind concepts and defences, stating they are not able to make the decisions any more because the power to fund support plans is controlled by managers who are have forgotten what it means to be face to face with the person.

As practice leaders we do not accept this argument.

If you can't see the person behind the decisions you are being presented with, then you need to stop and properly reflect. If you think the key decision you are involved in making is allocation of funding or the bestowing of services via a care plan, then you are just focusing on buying stuff. The key decisions are which values you are going to uphold, and which approach will underpin your practice and whether these will uphold the person's dignity and autonomy. Great social workers, the ones we value, are reflective both in and on action. They critique their intervention at the point of intervening, recalibrating their approach as they go to tailor and personalise their response to the person, ensuring that their voice is central to all decisions.

You are a social worker first, and to be a social worker you must live your life as such before you are employed as a professional social work practitioner. If we believe that social work is a vocation, a strong impulse or inclination to follow a path rather than just a career, then you must also understand that the social worker is who you are, not what you are. If you understand that when the job is not there the social worker inside still is, then you're on that journey.

💬 A skanking New Year

MARK HARVEY (with TYLER HARVEY)

It was New Year's Eve in Willow House. It hadn't been a happy Christmas, not like the ones Rudy had always known. Not now his dad wasn't at home with him.

This one had been loud but in the wrong way, without dancing and nice food and music. Rudy had cried a lot. He didn't want to, but he couldn't stop himself. This was the second Christmas Rudy had not liked and the second Christmas he had missed everything he and his dad used to do. It was never going be the same.

He hated that he didn't do the things they had done together any more. Christmas and New Year brought the best memories but now the worst times, with each year the memories making him sadder, nothing would ever feel the way it did.

Rudy sat hunched with anticipation at the makeshift desk in the dining room, staring at a computer his care home had set up recently. He had never been allowed to use a computer before; he'd asked for one many times, but had been told he wouldn't know how to use it even if he had one. He then suggested he could have a tablet like the ones in the adverts but all the manager, Vanessa, ever said was, 'I thought you'd be fed up of tablets with all the ones we give you' whilst laughing and strutting off. But now there was one here, a real computer, and one that Rudy could use. The problem was that it didn't seem to work.

Rudy did know that on computers you could find music, because he had seen it on the telly. But there wasn't one at home with Dad, so he wasn't quite sure what to do. His Dad had told him that the only true way to listen to music was on vinyl and mostly that's what they did with music, put records on and dance.

Music was what Rudy wanted now from this computer. He'd sat there for at least an hour pressing the buttons getting warning sounds and not much else; no music appeared, even less the music he wanted. Despite requesting help and the fact that he had been 'extra good' all day, as he saw it, the staff said they were too busy to help.

'I only want one choon,' he pleaded but no help came. 'You'll like it, better than shit you're playing.' Rudy motioned to the radio sitting on top of the TV, which also happened to be on but had the volume down, blaring what his Dad would have also called 'shit'.

'Rudy! That is unacceptable, if you swear again you will not be allowed on the computer,' said Vanessa sternly.

He kept trying, asking, waiting...like always, but no one was there to help.

'I'm getting a bit sick of your behaviour', said Vanessa. Rudy knew his good behaviour book would now mean nothing – a line to say he hadn't been well behaved would be scratched into it and the thought of this made him cry again.

'Rudy, that's it. Time's up, other people want to use the computer anyway.' Vanessa leaned in and switched the monitor off, before giving him a stone-cold look. Like an owl he stared with wide tearful eyes whilst she waited for a response.

'I...' he began but struggled for words. He was sad, angry and lonely but surrounded by people he didn't want to be near. That's why he needed his song.

'You can go back to your room if you need some space.' Vanessa began to force him out of the seat before he was ready. After part dragging and part guiding him up, she gestured him away. 'It's time to do your room chores', Vanessa said impatiently. 'Katie will help you.' And she gestured to a girl, shorter than Vanessa, standing in the doorway. Katie had long hair to the front and sides with the rest shaved short. She was just like the girls Rudy used to see at the New Year's Eve party, and like those girls, Katie always wore a Fred Perry polo – just like the ones Rudy used to get from his dad.

Every Christmas a new Fred Perry. Rudy always opened that first; he had every colour he wanted. Now he only had one, all the others had either been shrunk or mixed up with the other 'residents' clothes' and his last one was heading the same way. Once he had tried to get one of his polo's back from Kevin, but Kevin didn't give it back. He didn't tell Rudy why, he just didn't give it back and eventually this led to Rudy hitting Kevin, and then a meeting where he got told off... He never got his polo back.

He had asked the staff to buy him new ones with the money he had, but they always said, 'it wasn't in his best interests to spend that much on one T-shirt'. Instead he would go shopping to Asda where they would buy him polo shirts. These ones didn't have the leaves on the front that Rudy wanted; the leaves that he knew made them Fred Perry's.

Katie hadn't been at Willow House long, but she was different to the staff and Rudy liked her. He knew she was like him and his Dad.

'Ruuuuuude Gellllllllllllll!' Rudy shouted as he pointed at Katie.

Vanessa had had enough. 'Rudy! How many times do I have to tell you? We don't shout and that is inappropriate.'

'Oh Vanessa, I'll sort it out', Katie said, as she guided Rudy from the dining room and down the corridor towards his bedroom.

All Rudy really wanted was his Dad; he wanted him to sing and dance like he used to when he was sad. He wanted the music on the computer to make him feel happy again, he wanted to tell his dad what was wrong. He wanted that song his dad used to play to him when he knew Rudy was sad. He couldn't understand why this didn't happen.

When he first moved to Willow House, he used to sing his song loudly along with other tracks, but would often get told to keep it down by the staff. Especially Sue when she wanted to watch *EastEnders*.

Now he couldn't remember the words and he wondered if he would ever hear the song again. He felt like he had lost it, lost a part of him and his Dad. Two Christmases is a long time to never do the things you were used to. It's a long time to not be able to hug anyone at all.

'Rudy, don't cry', said Katie softly as they walked to his bedroom. 'What were you looking for on the computer anyway?'

'Dad's make Rudy happy song', he said as best he could.

'Oh', said Katie. 'Well you won't find anything on there, it's not connected to the Wi-Fi,' she said. 'What song is it anyway? I may have it.'

A sudden smile crept over Rudy's face, mischievous and perhaps almost knowing. He inhaled deeply before giving every word he spoke every inch of voice he had whilst pointing to Katie and laughing. 'Ruuuuuuude Geeeeelllllllllll!'

'Rudy, stop! You'll get into trouble again.' But she began to laugh delicately, attempting to conceal her amusement by covering her mouth with her hand. She knew what Rudy meant and he knew what he meant but none of the other staff had a clue.

Katie had tried to explain to them that he wasn't being inappropriate, but they would have none of it, telling her that if she wanted to become a social worker she would have to learn how to enforce boundaries.

Vanessa shouted from the dining room door, 'Room – now!'

Katie ushered Rudy down the bedroom corridor as fast as possible and entered his room. The door screeched a little as she opened it, and she gestured for him to go in first. He did as he was told, suddenly worried that Katie was going to tell him off like Vanessa. There wasn't much point in objecting as if he did not do what staff wanted it would be written in the be good behaviour book. He sat down onto his bed and looked blankly at the carpet.

'Are you okay, Rudy? You look...I don't know', she questioned.

The carpet was a dull brown from years of it being walked over, and no real care being given to it. It was hoovered, but never washed or scrubbed clean. Rudy sat for a moment, trying to think of what to say.

He thought and thought harder until he was ready and tried to muster the words into existence with everything he could manage. 'You...you're the same.' He sulked and turned away looking at the poster on his wall – the black and white chequers strongly contrasting the beige paint.

'No. No, that's not true. I just, I have to follow the rules, you know?'

Katie picked up the pile of washed T-shirts on the end of Rudy's bed and started to fold them.

'We can look for music on here if you want', she said, taking her phone out of her pocket.

He didn't really hear what she said; he wasn't listening. His attention was focused on his poster, the only poster he had from his old room, a poster that then made him think of his dad again and then that feeling in his tummy, the one that got worst at times.

'Rudy? What are you looking at?' She walked over whilst still folding an Asda polo shirt. She placed it onto his desk and knelt down next to him. 'Tell me what's wrong,' she said softly to Rudy. In that one sentence she took him back. His dad – that was what his dad would say when he was sad or angry.

'Make Rudy happy song', he said to Katie with a smile and started to try to sing. 'What wrong, what wrong? Tell me what wrong Rudy.'

Katie was struggling to understand what Rudy was saying but realised she had said something familiar to him. 'Is that your Dad's song, Rudy?'

Rudy just kept repeating, part singing part saying, 'What wrong, what wrong, tell me' as he started to bounce seated on his bed. It suddenly dawned on Katie what Rudy was saying and more importantly what song he was after. She walked over to Rudy's shelf and looked through a selection of CDs, trying to find what she knew he wanted. The CDs weren't his music taste though; last Christmas the staff had given presents out and he'd got a One Direction CD. He'd tried to dance to it but had decided as his dad would say, 'It's shit,' a statement that got him in to trouble with the staff and labelled him as ungrateful.

Katie flicked through, increasingly dejected by the CDs she saw in front of her. Half of them were still in the cellophane and certainly not what she thought Rudy would listen to anyway. Katie gave up and turned to Rudy clutching her phone. 'Music,' she said and showed him the Spotify logo on her screen. Katie sat next to Rudy and typed 'The Selecter' in the search box. She was fairly confident that she knew the song Rudy was after – one she herself had danced to many a time. She just hoped she was right.

Rudy had stopped bouncing on the bed and was now watching Katie's phone intensely. All of a sudden music started to play. Rudy was frozen for a moment and then screamed loudly, smiling and bouncing on his bed. From his reaction Katie knew she had found it.

The musical introduction seemed to energise Rudy. Bouncing turned to leg swinging on the edge of the bed, to standing and jumping, to full blown skanking. Katie was shocked at what she was seeing. He was good, energetic and loving every moment.

Rudy could not contain himself; this was the song that Dad sang to make him happy. Dad knew Rudy better than any person could ever know anyone. Dad knew when Rudy was sad and he knew what to do.

Lots of things could make Rudy sad and angry. Sometimes it was his Dad, turning the TV over or rushing him to get on the bus in the morning. Sometimes Rudy didn't know why he was sad or angry but every time his dad knew what to do. He would sing:

Oh won't you tell me
Oh won't you tell me
Won't you tell me
Tell me tell me what's wrong – 'Rudy'

If Rudy knew what was wrong, he would tell his dad as best he could whilst they sat on the sofa trying to regain their breath after such a dance outburst. More often than not he would just feel better and his dad would hug him.

Katie watched Rudy dance, loving every second of it, partly because she felt proud of herself for understanding what Rudy was after but also because Rudy was good. He knew his moves; he could just be another dancing rude boy at any of the gigs or club nights she went to.

As the track came to an end Katie clapped and Rudy bowed. 'My music', he said, pointing at the poster he was staring at earlier. 'Dad and Rudy.'

Katie looked up at the poster; it was an iconic image and one very familiar to her. A black and white chequer board pattern covered every edge of the poster with a large image of a man and woman dancing in the middle. The word 'Ska' was emblazoned in one corner and a Trojan warrior helmet in the other with the word 'sharp' encircling it. Across the bottom a date, time and venue for a New Year's Eve party: '31st Jan 1999–2000 The Broadway, A Skanking New Year!'

'Party', he said, with a grin creeping across his face. The Broadway was an old club his dad used to take him to every New Year's Eve, right up to the New Year party before he died. They would dance, or Skank as Rudy and his dad would say, laugh at each other and have fun. He hadn't been since his dad had gone; the closest he'd got was dancing alone in his room listening to 'shit' CDs.

Katie knew the venue; she had been there herself a few years back. However 'Skanking New Years' weren't an option any more: things were a little more dub step than two tone. Katie had an idea though; she grabbed her phone and showed Rudy a picture on Facebook. It had a black and white image of a group of young people dancing under a big logo announcing the 'Trojan Records' official New Year Club Night. Rudy didn't know what all the words meant but he knew the people and he certainly knew the orange Trojan helmet that made up the O of Trojan records.

'You wanna go?' Katie asked. Rudy nodded. She looked at the poster for a moment, thinking to herself. 'Leave it with me.' She took the poster down and removed the sticky tack from the back. 'Can I borrow it, Rudy?' she said.

He nodded. 'Yes you can', he said assertively. She delicately folded it in half and smiled at Rudy. The smile injected a nice feeling in Rudy, a small tinge of hope. He smiled back as she left his room.

Now alone, he sat staring at his feet. Thinking about his Dad, he started to cry again.

'Absolutely not.' Vanessa snatched the poster out of Katie's hand and threw it to one side. 'How irresponsible can you be?'

'But he must have gone with his Dad, that's why he has this poster in his room. He loved the music I just played him. He clearly knew it, he kinda asked for it', Katie said, slightly pleading.

'No.'

'Well, why not, Vanessa? I was going with my friends anyway, so I'll be there with him, he'll be safe', she pushed. The realisation that if she didn't make this happen then she would have let Rudy down started to weigh on her; those five minutes in his room showed her how much it meant to him.

'This is ridiculous!' snapped Vanessa. 'He won't be safe; he'll be a vulnerable adult in a vulnerable situation, and what if he hits someone?'

Katie picked up the poster and began to rashly fold it into even smaller pieces until all that was left was a messy square. 'It won't be like that', she pleaded. 'Anyway, me and my friends will be there.'

'For someone training to be a social worker you have a funny idea of professional boundaries and safeguarding. Risk assessments not mean anything to you? What do you do at university? Any way he is on a DoLS!'

Katie was getting angry herself now. What the hell did 'he was on a DoLS' have to do with it? But Vanessa carried on. 'You have a duty of care. Anyway, we only have night staff on at that time and he needs to be here for his medication.'

'How big are the fucking tablets that they can't fit in my bag?' Katie snapped.

Vanessa looked shocked and took a moment before spluttering an angry red-faced reply.

'Leave now. I don't want to hear any more about it, and I don't want him getting any ideas.' She tossed the poster on the desk and ushered Katie out of the office.

The door closed in Katie's face, and she exhaled her disappointment and her breath, inches from the door, bounced back against her pale face. She was conscious that she was now going to be in trouble with the university and had possibly lost her placement. She could have kicked herself for getting angry.

'Yes?' She heard Rudy's empty voice behind her, the voice with continual disappointment that knew the disappointment was not going to stop. She took a deep breath before turning to face him, his eyes glaring in hope whilst waiting for an answer he now knew he probably didn't want to hear.

She couldn't do it to him. 'Yes. Yes, we are going to go tonight. I will come back at 9 p.m. for you.' She grabbed a piece of paper from a nearby table and drew a clock face with 9 pm showing on it. 'We will need to be quick though, so... So go and get ready now and make sure you're good to go when I appear. Wear your favourite polo shirt, eh? I'll get your meds...and...and I'll sort us a lift with my friend Marcy, but we need to be quick when I arrive. Okay?'

Katie pawed at her phone, messaging her friend and co-clubber for the night, Marcy. 'We have an extra dancer to pick up tonight here is the address' read the short message.

Rudy stood stunned, paralysed with shock and excitement.

He snapped out of it, and ran to his room, practically leaping the whole way in two steps to get ready for the best New Year's Eve in years.

It felt like forever for Rudy, who waited in his room until it was the correct time. He then walked to the front window and saw a car pull up outside, Katie stepped out.

Quietly opening the front door, she saw Rudy and rushed him out, careful not to make any noise, before pulling the door shut slowly and delicately.

She turned and surveyed the area trying to find Rudy, who had already jumped into Marcy's car. He then to her dismay shouted,

'Ruuuuuuuuude Gelllllllllll!' from the back seat. Her face dropped, and a light appeared from the office window as a curtain was drawn back.

She ran to the car, slamming the door shut behind her. 'Okay– Okay we need to go!' she said, looking back over her shoulder to see Vanessa's face, full of fury, looking out of the window.

But it was done, and her face faded as the car began to drive toward a new, old adventure for Rudy – toward the memory Rudy has been trying to relive for two years.

Katie felt exhilarated and petrified at the same time. She thought about the ramifications of her actions and the list of crimes Vanessa would read out at her midway, that's if she even made it that far:

aiding someone to abscond,

placing a vulnerable person at risk,

safeguarding and breaching a DoLS

but the 'Train to Skaville' cries interspersed by 'Ruuuuuude Geeeeellllll' and 'Ruuuuuude Booooooooooyyyy' coming from behind her seemed to help.

The uni and social services bang on about strength-based work and using community assets. What was more strength based than Rudy's excellent skanking? Better than most of the blokes she knew and after all this was her community: a Ska Community, the best community asset she knew about. Better than a One Direction CD in your bedroom anyway.

As they drove down Ealing Broadway the cries of 'Ruuuuuuuuude Booooooooyyyyy' and a heavy beat turned every head in the street. It was going to be a Skanking New Year after all.

The reclaiming of radical social work

We love the idea of being activists: radicals with a cause creating new futures in partnership with people whose lives we are invited to be a part of. Social work attracted us to it as it felt radical, edgy and different, reflected the culture of the homes we studied in and allowed us endless opportunity to debate in the halls of the colleges and universities we grew up in. There was an element of romanticism that attracted us to these models of social work and the writings of Roy Bailey and Mike Brake (1975) and others. Radical social work, we imagined, strived to improve people's lives by supporting frontline activists who were struggling to maintain a radical perspective. As Billy Bragg fans, the idea of being active with the activists held huge appeal. Social work had us hooked; it drew us in.

In these radical social workers, we could see the conversations that happened around us throughout our childhood growing up: ward party meetings, debates and days spent at marches and rallies with our parents, arguing politics over Sunday lunch, nights without sleep watching the results of televised elections. We especially loved the marches; the police officers always seemed to have a ready supply of sweets that they willingly shared with all the kids. The trouble was that when we started to become involved with social work training and education, we were told that our type of radical social work was taught as being a thing of the past, an intervention that actually had no intervention which defined it and made it replicable across other social work settings, its only focus to radicalise the oppressed and shout a bit louder. As we left these conversations, we felt deflated, left with a feeling that we had somehow missed the boat, had been out of time with our view that social work was radical in nature had a very brief moment and been proven to be ineffective and that the world had moved onto embrace the more structured form of practice that the care management reforms of the 1990s had introduced.

We have often pondered the fate of our version of social work, social work as a radical agent in the system, and the impact it had, if any, on modern social care systems and social work practice. The rise of care management would suggest that radical social work had very little impact as an enabler of equality. The case management model heralded the end of the early drivers of social work practice and the core relational, radical model of social work which had dominated throughout the 1970s and 1980s. People become cases. Conversations became assessments. Social workers became the professionals. Family support became multi-disciplinary team meetings and family group conferences. The need for human-to-human contact became reframed as transference of risk from the case to the professional. The multi-disciplinary team helped transfer that risk so that no one was accountable for the outcome of the case. For us, it seemed that we had lost a sense of proportionality; we had forgotten that the roots of social work were in a social model. Case management approaches looked at the individual as the source of risk and required change, without considering wider societal constructs and structural inequalities which shaped and sustained the individual's distress. From this model of case management, the seeds of care management seem to have grown. Developed as the ideal approach to manage the professional risk transferred through case management, care management delivers commissioned, prescription-based care and risk management which focuses on need at the level of the individual. This is not in a way that allows for self-empowerment and choice but one that meets perceived self-failure with risk aversion and control dressed up as meeting need. The much-maligned NHS and Community Care Act 1990 served in many people's eyes as the legal bludgeon that forced through these new approaches. At its heart was the first major attempt to reform care and introduce the small steps towards inclusion. It did, however, herald the dawn of care management, with social workers as the professional tool within the multi-disciplinary team managing risk through assessments which led to the commissioning of risk-mitigating support plans. The industrialisation of social care was well and truly born.

If radical social work had anything positive to offer, surely we would have seen it shaping care management and, more importantly, the ability of people it worked with to live the lives they wanted. The core concept of radical social work was to tell the person you worked with to 'man the barricades' and demand their rights; the social work role was to stand right there next to them. However, too often in social work education this rich tradition of social work is reduced to a single lesson, perhaps just 45 minutes in length: what could be a detailed analysis of social work's role in resisting oppression and ensuring equality reduced to nothing more than, 'Well, we have to mention it in the syllabus.'

To a certain extent the social work educationalists and academics are correct in recognising the marginalising of radical social work in the era of dominant care management approaches. Social work education is under great pressure to prepare social workers to be ready to practise within the dominant cultures of the social work employers students graduate to. Radical social work is understood by most social work employers as a purely political concept which is of historical interest, but lacking relevance to current practice. What this argument seems to miss, or perhaps be consciously unwilling to acknowledge, was that the idea of radical social work had permeated much more than giving a narrow political message. The radical social work approaches set a firm foundation for some of the concepts we now take for granted. Person-centred practice is by nature radical in that it requires the social worker to be singularly minded in upholding the person's right for their voice, their wishes, feelings and beliefs to be central to decision making. Social work with adults starts from the premise that the adult's capacity for self-determination is enshrined in their human rights and written into the statutory principles of the Mental Capacity Act 2005.

If social work education is to remain relevant to practice with adults there is a need for greater creativity in how social work academics engage with frontline practice (Ferguson 2017) and an enhanced level of legal literacy in human rights underpinning the curricula. Debate is needed to explore questions such as: is social work a scientific method which students can be trained in the application of, or is it more of a creative art form? Good social work practitioners continually reflect on and refine their values to ensure their practice remains ethical; do they do this through scientific method or through creative expression? Is the better social practice a blend of both the scientific and the artistic in a new form of creative expression? There are ethically important questions which should/must run through social work about the nature of relationships and power dynamics between social workers and the people they support. Creative approaches which inclusively invite a diverse audience into social work expand the edges of practice. How well we collaborate to build research outcomes into these creative processes of new knowledge generation about the nature of social work will determine how likely new ideas are integrated into the way that social workers practise in the future.

The radical social work we aspired toward, however, is no longer the answer to inspiring creativity at the edges of social work practice. The version of politicised radical social work we grew up with and which first attracted us to the profession was of its time; it stood apart precisely because it was at the edge of the conventions of social work practice. By nature, it is no longer radical. The term radical seems to have shifted from its natural descriptor 'believing or expressing the belief that there should be great or extreme social change' to one that describes radical approaches as characterised by a departure from tradition: innovative or progressive change. The shift of radical ideas in health and social care seems now to be the domain of management models and a way of re-branding change programmes. At its core, this tips a nod to the traditions of the past. Radical thinking of previous decades is often what has defined current policy; think personalisation, advocacy, human rights as a core to practice and the foundation of all modern care law. But now there are dedicated NHS websites calling for the radicalisation of its staff and offering training on how to be radical with a School for Health and Care Radicals. There is nothing wrong with this organisational approach to new ideas; however, organisationally owned and led ideas can never be truly radical. That is not to say you cannot have radical ideas from within health and social care and implement them, but this is generally done despite the system not because of it. Radical ideas from practitioners grow and challenge the system; they cannot be commissioned by it. The modern penchant for reactive, short-term responses to perceived wicked questions within health and social care is as far removed from any idea of radical thinking as you can get yet seems to want to wholly align itself to the concept, or at least the terminology. The radicals have become fully integrated into the status quo and radical is now the new normal. Somehow, to become radical has been co-opted by the mainstream, branded and monetised into a more compliant form of change agent educated by an NHS-funded school for self-proclaimed 'new radicals' with an agenda to 'deviate, disrupt and transform' (Bevan and Fairman 2014). For the social work employer, the successful co-option of radicals into business as usual marks successful survival of another stage in the continued dominance of corporate risk mitigation through care management. We feel a strange sense of discomfort, which emerges from deep inside us, when we find ourselves listening to a senior manager or national social work leader introduce themselves as a radical social worker but then go on to explain that what radical means to them is what we believe every social worker should do. There is nothing radical in being person-centred; it's what we are supposed to do. If radical is no longer pushing the boundaries, testing the edges of social work practice, is it time for a new approach to emerge?

In a social work practice world where radical social work no longer exists something slightly different may be filling the void. Something that can be described as the rise of the new social work bohemians, partly because we love a good name, but more importantly because the history of the bohemian movement is increasingly reflected in this branch of social work. The new bohemians seek to position themselves as a more authentic form of responsive, critically reflective organisational leaders, nurturing cultures based on trust at the leadership level to encourage questioning, and challenging in their everyday conversations and actions the status quo to drive innovation through frontline social worker self-organising activism (Webber Shandwick 2014). Lyn Romeo, the UK Government's Chief Social Worker for Adults in England, has developed a new vision for social work with adults, calling on social workers to take back and own their own destiny for practice, and drive community social work and strengths-based approaches which reconnect with the relational practices of the past. The question, 'Is social work an art or a science?' is at the heart of the reimagining of social work practice with adults. Our answer is that social work is both: a profession based on scientific method and rigour in its approach towards research and evidence generation which also recognises the power of qualitative evidence generated from working alongside people to effect change. Social work requires artistic responses and freedom of thinking to create something new with people, to imagine new futures and the acts required to bring them into being. More importantly it requires a capacity for love in its infinite forms, the acceptance of humans as unique individuals that may require a truly creative relationship to overcome the rigid and structural discriminations within society.

Whilst inequality in society has been a constant, its inherent discriminations ebb and wane in their public support. At a time where there appears to be an increased tolerance of ill-informed and stereotyped discrimination, let alone an outward application of principles – dressed up as political viewpoints – which are arguably abhorrent to social work values, you will generally see the rise of bohemianism. This is predominantly in the arts and historically in youth and community development culture but now increasingly in the new social work movements and ethos: a collective of practitioners committed to ideas of equality in their truest form, creatively shaping a social work response in the post-Care Act world, seeking to end the incarceration and commodification of people.

In a world where the delivery of social care and social work is tougher than we have experienced before, you see something new emerging. There is a clear momentum of creative social work, in part embedded in the old heart of social work but driven by a new desire; an enhanced application and will to create. With creative references drawn from new science, music and other performing arts, social work practice is changing and joining these creative bohemian opportunities.

The growth of social media and the ability to connect is a key driver in these new ideas. Now not only can social work across the UK start to connect and share but social work across the world is beginning to influence at an international level. The art of the blog has been harnessed by many to share new ideas and thinking, no longer shackled by the dogma and rigidity of a singular academic approach but driven by a passion to shape and harness something new in our profession, casting a nod to the 17th- to 19th-century pamphlet writers, seeking equality and citizenship at the individual and community level, influencing policy and direct action. Across the internet you can see growth in the insightful and critically reflective commentary which is emerging about social work and social care. All of these offerings can only be relevant if you are open and reflexive, able to integrate the insights of others to help reshape and deepen your own understanding about the reality people face and live every day.

The marking of a life taken, embodied in the creative expression which led to the Justice for LB quilt, is yet another reminder of the power of art to elicit deep emotional responses and drive a passion for better social work. Connor Sparrowhawk drowned whilst being detained for the purposes of care and treatment in an NHS Trust hospital in England. Social workers were involved in his life from an early age through to the admission to the hospital where he died. His mother, Sara Ryan, had been writing blogs about her 'daft life'; these became a live narrative account of the trauma she experienced and her fight as she campaigned for justice. We followed the campaign every step of the way, reflecting on what we understood about our own approach to practice as a result of knowing Sara and her family's story. We have had the privilege of seeing and experiencing the quilt in real life. The impact is difficult to describe. The quilt defines the pain and loss felt by the loss of Connor. Yet somehow it also celebrates his life. It is a form of creative expression that will not let a young man's death be forgotten or unanswered. The stories and creativity of Sara Ryan's photography capture images which reflect a humanity that shapes and reshapes our social work practice. We must understand that statements of person-centred and radical practice from social workers are meaningless if they do nothing to genuinely uphold people's rights to live lives filled with colour of creative expression, love and happiness in all its diversity of meaning.

For us, social media platforms such as Twitter have played a huge part in not just sustaining our knowledge and learning at a real level but have connected us to a wider network of social workers and inspirational people in the social care world, including initiating the collective which has formed to write this book. Collectively we are striving to develop something new, something shaped by people not done unto them. We started this with our blogs, then moved on to curating more critically reflective, creative conversations such as tweet chats which were co-hosted with online nurse community networks and through calls to action made through the English Adult Principal Social Worker Network. The first of these calls to action asked social workers to share through a creative image or text posted on the social media platform Twitter an example of where they had in their daily lives made a decision which others may argue was unwise (James *et al.* 2017). As curators of this conversation, we set out to highlight the ludicrous subjectivity that many public sector professionals apply to their practice and how that contrasts with the values that apply to their own decision making. The social workers who engaged with the call shared their unwise decisions about chocolate, sex or alcohol. This was not a flippant piece of publicising but one that highlighted the perceived worth of people by some that would refuse such a life for others. Alongside the call to action, across the country adult Principal Social Workers ran post-qualifying social work practice development sessions which provided for a safe space where social workers could explore and challenge the boundaries and edges of their own practice. The key was a collective act across the country at the same time, not to get people to follow the law – although that would have been a great by-product – but to encourage and nurture the idea beyond the perception that people are allowed by law to make unwise decisions, to instil the idea that creativity in social work practice makes self-determination a reality.

Many a self-proclaimed modern 'radial social worker' will tell you they are because of their drive to promote person-centred approaches and deliver choice and control. No, sorry: that is your job not a radical approach. If we believe radical is doing what we are supposed to do, then it is no wonder that the term has been hijacked and used as confirmation of the new 'change management style'.

Better social work happens when social workers recognise the fundamental principles of human rights and equality, and that these are protected in national and international law, positive obligations to uphold the conventions and policies which frame their practice. They ensure these principles underpin their approach to social work. Social workers understand the importance of using and contributing to case law and applying these rights in their own practice. They understand the effects of oppression, discrimination and poverty. They recognise the contribution of social work to promoting social justice, inclusion and equality and are receptive to the idea that there may be conflicts in the social work role between promoting rights and enforcing responsibilities.

Obviously, the world of social media can also attract those in our profession who cannot see beyond the negatives, engaging in a self-promoting downward spire of doom. Do not get us wrong; debate and questioning are excellent, indeed vital, to enable the continued growth of the job many of us love. However, the trap of critiquing continually without suggesting solutions or responsibility will only play out in your practice and wellbeing.

Social work has to be so much more than the application of legislation if it is to remain relevant. It has also to embrace the responsibility it has to people; a responsibility it is granted by society, not one it owns to deliver. We can and should hold on to the very elements that took us on this journey in the first place, celebrating all that was right in the social work models of the past and merging them with not just the evidence of today's research but the desires and creativity of people's aspirations, assets and strengths. Social work does not have an automatic right to enter living rooms, walk the streets, sit on park benches and at people's bedsides. Knowing and delivering much more than the forms you clutch has to be a given or you have no right being there. Indeed, if we proffer forms and abdicate the responsibility of our role to citizens our profession will die.

Modern social work is well placed and key to understanding and mitigating the inherent failings of reactive ideas, policy and commissioning that trip up its own outcome due to narrow thinking. The ability to understand beyond the systems, yet work within them, moulding what is good with what is progressive, is an art. An art that social work can bring. One that should be inherent whether you are a case-holding frontline worker, a manager or any other role. We are a single profession, defined as such not by a qualification but a common value base and belief. If you haven't taken those steps towards the positive new age of social work or if you have drifted from its path, then come and join in.

Social work has to be part of the solution. In a time when we are desperate for strong professionals with a will to fight positively through dark days, we need to respond. It's too easy to become the negative face of adversity when times are tough. Social workers face potentially unbearable levels of complexity which can have a powerful impact on their personal as well as professional identities (Ferguson 2017). We often hear social workers arguing that we need social work in every area to put right what is wrong in society. Now we may be misinterpreting the intent behind this argument, but it is deeply flawed. We are not the custodians of society, there for risk to be transferred onto as if we hold a greater position in societal hierarchies; rather, we need to learn to be part of it, in fact we need to ask humbly if we can come and play again. Then and only then can we work alongside people on an equal footing and create opportunity, not risk-averse application that does to, rather than with or for, the person. That's why we need to join and start to be part of the solution.

Conclusion

In this chapter we have argued that in order to keep social work relevant we need to reclaim the profession by paying attention to creative approaches which innovate and improve our relationships with the people we are here to serve. We would argue that a bohemian movement in social work is positive, progressive creatives with a humanist understanding of the art of people, cultures, love and a dash of science to add colour. You are a social worker first and live your life as such before you are employed as a social worker. If you believe that social work is a vocation, a strong impulse or inclination to follow a path rather than just a career, then you must also understand that the social worker is who you are, not what you are. If you understand that when the job's not there the social worker inside still is, then you're on that journey. There is not one type of social worker or one purest value base that makes us a single homogenous breed of either activists or state tools. The future of social work is a collective of those who wish to create and contribute by doing something new, something beyond the rigidity of the purest models of the past and the pressure of the money or lack of: creating with citizens, getting in deep with the messy stuff, making the tears bearable, the opportunity real, the ends of life the best they can be and the next generations ready to drive us forward. Our hope is that having read this you will want to embrace your creativity; go out and start creating.

Suggested further reading and resources

Fenton, J. (2016) *Values in Social Work: Reconnecting with Social Justice* (Reshaping Social Work). London: Palgrave.

Recommended Resources

Blogs and social media accounts

The original versions of our blogs that we have featured in this book are freely available at lastquangoinhalifax (https://lastquangoinhalifax.wordpress.com) and mwharvey's blog Social Work, Billy Bragg, Biggles, The Great Leap and everything (https://mwharveyblog.wordpress.com).

We have been heavily influenced to make changes and incorporate human rights into our practice by the lived experiences of parents of disabled young people and adults who have written about their family's lives. Mark Neary @MarkNeary1, father of Steven Neary, blogs at Love, Belief and Balls (https://markneary1dotcom1.wordpress.com/about) about his experiences of social care. Mark Brown @Markliamb, father of Mikey, blogs at The Tired Optimist (https://thetiredoptimist.wordpress.com). Sara Ryan @sarasiobhan, mother of Connor Sparrowhawk, maintains a blog at My Daft Life (https://mydaftlife.com). For a human rights perspective on closing the gap between theoretical rights and lived reality we would suggest that you follow Neil Crowther @neilmcrowther (https://makingrightsmakesense.wordpress.com).

The Chief Social Workers in England both maintain a social media presence and will engage with contacts from across the profession. The Chief Social Worker for Adults, Lyn Romeo @LynRomeo_CSW, regularly publishes a blog which provides links to reports and other resources (https://lynromeo.blog.gov.uk). You can also follow the Chief Social Worker for Children, Isabelle Trowler @IsabelleTrowler.

For informed perspectives on mental health and mental capacity law we recommend that you follow the blog sites produced by mental capacity researcher Lucy Series @TheSmallPlaces (http://thesmallplaces.blogspot.co.uk), police officer Michael Brown @MentalHealthCop (https://mentalhealthcop.wordpress.com) and The Masked AMHP @MaskedAMHP (http://themaskedamhp.blogspot.co.uk).

To keep up to date with current issues in the profession, we recommend you follow @CommunityCare (www.communitycare.co.uk).

Websites
Stay Up Late

All author proceeds from this book are going to the charity Stay Up Late, whose work is hugely influential on us and how we practise. You can find out more about the charity at their website (https://stayuplate.org) including details of how to volunteer and get out to more gigs as a gig buddy, pairing up and becoming friends with a learning disabled person (https://stayuplate.org/gig-buddies-project). There are a number of gig buddy schemes running across England.

Rightful Lives

Rightful Lives is an online exhibition which is curated by parents of learning disabled and autistic people in England. It explores the theme of human rights and people with autism and/or learning disabilities. The idea for the exhibition came about through a conversation between the parents, human rights lawyers, journalists, social workers and academics working in disability studies about how the legal framework of the Human Rights Act seems to barely touch the lives of people with learning disabilities. In May 2018, the curators put out a call to arms asking for contributions from anyone interested in human rights for learning disabled people. The responses are available at their website (http://rightfullives.net).

Legal websites

There are a number of really interesting websites which are useful starting points to help you keep up to date with current issues and debates in case law, including links to the original rulings.

Luke Clements is a good place to find resources around community care law and the Care Act 2014 (www.lukeclements. co.uk). The Centre for Adults' Social Care Advice Information and Dispute Resolution (www.cascaidr.org.uk), which is managed by Belinda Schwehr (www.schwehroncare.co.uk), also provides useful resources for considering fairness and legal principle in adults' health and social care services.

For case summaries on mental health and mental capacity law it is worth following 39 Essex Street who produce a monthly newsletter (www.39essex.com), and Mental Health Law Online (http://mentalhealthlaw.co.uk).

The British and Irish Legal Information Institute (BAILII) provides access to the most comprehensive set of British and Irish primary legal materials that are freely available online so you can source original case rulings (www.bailii.org).

Research and academic journals

We recommend you get (or stay) in the habit of keeping up to date with research. Websites like the Social Care, Learning Disabilities, Mental Health and Commissioning Elves (www.nationalelfservice. net/social-care) provide accessible summaries and analysis of newly published research. Research in Practice also publishes summaries of case law and research on social work practice with children (www. rip.org.uk) and social work practice with adults (www.ripfa.org.uk). The British Association of Social Workers publishes reports and position statements on its website (www.basw.co.uk). They also produce a regular magazine for members, *Professional Social Work* (www.basw.co.uk/resources/professional-social-work-psw). You can follow the Chief Executive of BASW, Ruth Allen @ruthallenonline.

Universities and other research organisations publish open access research reports, position papers or other resources based on their research (that may later be published in academic journals or books). These can be accessed from research-orientated centres such as the Centre for Disability Research at Lancaster (https://wp.lancs. ac.uk/cedr), the Centre for Critical Psychology and Education i-human project (http://ihuman.group.shef.ac.uk) at Sheffield, the Joseph Rowntree Foundation (www.jrf.org.uk), the Centre for Welfare Reform (www.centreforwelfarereform.org) and the Norah Fry Centre for Disability Studies at the University of Bristol (www. bristol.ac.uk/sps/research/centres/norahfryresearch).

You can also sign up for new content alerts from journals like *Disability & Society* (www.tandfonline.com/loi/cdso20), *The British Journal of Social Work* (https://academic.oup.com/bjsw), *Social Work Education* (www.tandfonline.com/loi/cswe20) and *Practice: Social Work in Action* (www.basw.co.uk/resources/practice-social-work-action). Some articles are funded to be open access; however, if you want to access something which is closed, you can contact authors directly for copies of their 'author accepted manuscripts' (final draft version) which most publishers allow them to share for free.

Case law

A NHS Trust v P & Anor [2013] EWHC 50 (COP), accessed on 11/07/2019 at www.39essex.com/cop_cases/a-nhs-trust-v-p-anor

AM v SLAM NHS Foundation Trust [2013] UKUT 365 (AAC) (2013), accessed on 04/03/2019 at www.bailii.org/uk/cases/UKUT/AAC/2013/365.html

CH v A Metropolitan Council [2017] EWCOP 12, accessed on 04/03/2019 at www. bailii.org/ew/cases/EWCOP/2017/12.html

Engel and Others v The Netherlands 5100/71 [1976] ECHR 3 (1976), accessed 04/04/2019 at www.worldlii.org/eu/cases/ECHR/1976/3.html

Essex County Council v RF & Ors (Deprivation of Liberty and Damage) [2015] EWCOP 1 (2015), accessed on 15/07/2019 at www.bailii.org/ew/cases/EWCOP/2015/1. html

Guzzardi v Italy 7367/76 [1980] ECHR 5 (1980), accessed on 04/03/2019 at www. bailii.org/eu/cases/ECHR/1980/5.html

HL v The United Kingdom 45508/99 (2004) ECHR 471, accessed on 11/07/2019 at www.bailii.org/eu/cases/ECHR/2004/471.html

King's College Hospital NHS Foundation Trust v C & Anor [2015] EWCOP 80 (2015), accessed on 15/07/2019 at www.bailii.org/ew/cases/EWCOP/2015/80.html

KK v STCC [2012] EWCOP 2136 (2012), accessed on 04/03/2019 at www.bailii.org/ ew/cases/EWCOP/2012/2136.html

Local Authority X v MM & Anor (No. 1) [2007] EWHC 2003 (Fam), accessed on 04/03/2019 at www.bailii.org/ew/cases/EWHC/Fam/2007/2003.html

London Borough of Hillingdon v Neary & Anor [2011] EWCOP 1377 (2011), accessed on 04/03/2019 at www.bailii.org/ew/cases/EWHC/COP/2011/1377.html

P (by his litigation friend the Official Solicitor) *v Cheshire West and Chester Council & Anor; and P & Q* (by their litigation friend the Official Solicitor) *v Surrey County Council* [2014] UKSC 19 (2014), accessed on 11/07/2019 at www.bailii.org/uk/cases/UKSC/2014/19.html

P v Surrey County Council & Surrey Downs CCG [2015] EWCOP 54, accessed on 04/03/2019 at www.39essex.com/cop_cases/p-v-surrey-county-council-and-surrey-downs-ccg/

P & Q v Surrey County Council; sub nom Re MIG and MEG [2011] EWCA Civ 190, accessed on 04/03/2019 at www.bailii.org/ew/cases/EWCA/Civ/2011/190.html

PH & A local authority v Z limited & R [2011] EWHC 1704, accessed on 04/03/2019 at www.bailii.org/ew/cases/EWCOP/2011/1704.html

Re X (Court of Protection Practice) [2015] EWCA Civ 599, [2015] MHLO 44, accessed on 04/03/2019 at www.bailii.org/ew/cases/EWCA/Civ/2015/599.html

Rochdale Metropolitan Borough Council v KW & Ors (Rev 1) [2014] EWCOP 45 (2014), accessed on 04/03/2019 at www.bailii.org/ew/cases/EWCOP/2014/45.html

Sheffield City Council v E & Anor [2004] EWHC 2808 (Fam), accessed on 04/04/2019 at www.bailii.org/ew/cases/EWHC/Fam/2004/2808.html

SR v A Local Authority & Anor [2018] EWCOP 36, accessed on 04/03/2019 at www.bailii.org/ew/cases/EWCOP/2018/36.html

Stanev v Bulgaria [2012] ECHR 46, accessed on 04/03/2019 at www.escr-net.org/sites/default/files/caselaw/decision_on_stanev_v._bulgaria_0.pdf

Westminster City Council v Sykes [2014] EWCOP B9 (2014), accessed on 22/11/2018, at www.bailii.org/ew/cases/EWHC/COP/2014/B9.html

Winterwerp v The Netherlands [1979] ECHR 4, accessed on 04/03/2019 at www.bailii.org/eu/cases/ECHR/1979/4.html

Wye Valley NHS Trust v B (Rev 1) [2015] EWCOP 60 (2015), accessed on 04/03/2019 at www.bailii.org/ew/cases/EWCOP/2015/60.html

Glossary

Advocacy – receiving support from another person to help an individual express their wishes, feelings and beliefs.

Approved Mental Health Professional (AMHP) – a mental health professional who has been approved by a local authority in England to undertake specific duties under the Mental Health Act (Amended) 2007.

Assessment and Treatment Unit (ATU) – a secured, locked hospital that assesses and provides treatment for people's mental health needs. ATUs can be run by either the NHS or by a private provider. In England, the NHS is responsible for the quality of the care and treatment people in ATUs experience, regardless of which organisation runs the ATU.

Best Interest Assessor (BIA) – a social worker, nurse, occupational therapist or psychologist who has qualified in a professional role outlined within the Deprivation of Liberty Safeguards. Working with a mental health assessor, they arrange for assessments to be completed which determine whether someone is able to consent to arrangements that deprive them of their liberty and whether the arrangements are necessary and proportionate.

Case notes – the notes taken by a social worker (or other health and social care professional) which record their perspective on the contact they have had with the person.

Citizenship – the status conferred on a person by a state which recognises their citizenship of that country.

Deprivation of Liberty Safeguards (DoLS) – a set of procedural safeguards which form part of the Mental Capacity Act 2005, which ensure that a person who lacks capacity to consent to arrangements that deprive them of their liberty in a hospital or care home are able to access speedy judicial review and advocacy to review if the arrangements are necessary and proportionate.

European Convention on Human Rights (ECHR) – an international convention to protect human rights and political freedoms in Europe. Drafted in 1950 by the then newly formed Council of Europe, the Convention entered into force on 3 September 1953.

Human rights – the basic rights and freedoms that belong to every person in the world, from birth until death. They can never be taken away, although they can sometimes be restricted; for example, if a person breaks the law, or in the interests of national security.

Learning disability – this is defined within the World Health Organization international classification of diseases as a group of disorders that affect a person's ability to learn or process specific types of information which is in contrast to his/her apparent level of intellect.

Mental capacity – being able to understand, retain, weigh up options and communicate your wishes, feelings and beliefs.

Mental health – emotional, psychological and social wellbeing. The World Health Organization international classification of diseases defines mental and behavioural disorders as being a clinically recognisable set of symptoms or behaviours associated in most cases with distress and with interference with personal functions.

Newly qualified social worker (NQSW) – a registered social worker in England who is usually not more than two years post-qualifying. NQSWs are eligible to be offered an Assessed, Supported Year in Employment by social work employers.

Risk enablement – also known as positive risk taking, is an approach which recognises that risk is not only an inevitable part of life but often a welcome and necessary one.

Safeguarding – for the purposes of this book, safeguarding relates to adults who are in receipt of care and support services, who are at risk of harm or abuse and lack mental capacity.

Supervision – in keeping with the British Association of Social Workers UK supervision policy, supervision is a regular, planned, accountable process for all social workers, which must provide a supportive environment for reflecting on practice and making well-informed decisions using professional judgement and discretion.

Supported living – in keeping with the Care Quality Commission guidance on housing with care, supported living is defined as being schemes that provide personal care to people as part of the support that they need to live in their own homes. The personal care is provided under separate contractual arrangements to those for the person's housing. The accommodation is often shared but can be single household.

United Nations Convention on the Rights of Persons with Disabilities (UNCRDP) – the Convention on the Rights of Persons with Disabilities and its Optional Protocol (A/RES/61/106) was adopted on 13 December 2006 at the United Nations Headquarters in New York and was opened for signature on 30 March 2007. The Convention is intended as a human rights instrument with an explicit, social development dimension. It adopts a broad categorisation of persons with disabilities and reaffirms that all persons with all types of disabilities must enjoy all human rights and fundamental freedoms. It clarifies and qualifies how all categories of rights apply to persons with disabilities and identifies areas where adaptations have to be made for persons with disabilities to effectively exercise their rights and areas where their rights have been violated, and where protection of rights must be reinforced.

Wellbeing – in keeping with the New Economics Foundation, wellbeing is understood as being how people feel and how they function, both on a personal and a social level, and how they evaluate their lives as a whole.

Bibliography

A NHS Trust v P & Anor [2013] EWHC 50 (COP). Accessed on 11/07/2019 at www.39essex.com/cop_cases/a-nhs-trust-v-p-anor

ADASS (Association of Directors of Adult Social Services) (2012) Social Work in Adult Social Services. Accessed on 06/03/2019 at www.adass.org.uk/AdassMedia/stories/Workforce_Development/advicenote1.pdf

Agran, M. and Hughes, C. (2013) '"You can't vote – you're mentally incompetent": denying democracy to people with severe disabilities.' *Research and Practice for Persons with Severe Disabilities 38*, 58–62.

Allen, R. (2018) 'Welcome new social workers the world really needs you!' *Professional Social Work*, September 2018.

AM v SLAM NHS Foundation Trust [2013] UKUT 365 (AAC), [2013] MHLO 80, accessed on 04/03/2019 at www.bailii.org/uk/cases/UKUT/AAC/2013/365.html

Arendt, H. (2017) *The Origins of Totalitarianism* (later edition reprint). London: Penguin.

Argyris, C. (1990) *Overcoming Organizational Defences: Facilitating Organizational Learning*. Boston, MA: Allyn and Bacon.

Argyris, C. and Schön, D. (1978) *Organizational Learning*. Reading, MA: Addison Wesley.

Bailey, R. and Brake, M. (1975) *Radical Social Work*. London: Edward Arnold.

BASW (British Association of Social Workers) (2011) UK Supervision Policy. Accessed on 06/03/2019 at www.basw.co.uk/system/files/resources/basw_73346-6_0.pdf

BASW (British Association of Social Workers) (2012) The Code of Ethics for Social Work. Accessed on 06/03/2019 at www.basw.co.uk/about-basw/code-ethics

BASW (British Association of Social Workers) and Shaping Our lives (2016a) Disabled Adults and Social Workers: Charter. Accessed on 06/03/2019 at www.basw.co.uk/resources/disabled-adults-and-social-workers-charter

BASW (British Association of Social Workers) and Shaping Our lives (2016b) Disabled Adults and Social Workers: Position Statement. Accessed on 06/03/2019 at www.basw.co.uk/resources/disabled-adults-and-social-workers-position-statement

Beckett, S. (2009/1951) *Molloy*. London: Faber and Faber.

Beckman, L. (2007) 'Political equality and the disenfranchisement of people with intellectual impairments.' *Social Policy and Society 6*, 1, 13–23.

Bevan, H. and Fairman S. (2014) The New Era of Thinking and Practice in Change and Transformation: A Call to Action for Leaders of Health and Care. Accessed on 28.02.2018 at www.england.nhs.uk/improvement-hub/publication/change-and-transformation-white-paper/

Bowling, A. (2017) *Measuring Health: A Review of Subjective Health, Well-Being and Quality of Life Measurement Scales*, Fourth Edition. London: Open University Press.

Bridges, W. (2004) *Transitions: Making Sense of Life's Changes*, Revised 25th Anniversary Edition. Cambridge, MA: Da Capo Press.

British Medical Association (1978) 'The Normansfield Inquiry.' *British Medical Journal 2*, 1560–1563. Accessed on 06/03/2019 at www.ncbi.nlm.nih.gov/pmc/articles/PMC1608780/pdf/brmedj00155-0050.pdf

Brown, M., James, E. and Hatton, C. (2017) A Trade in People: The Inpatient Healthcare Economy for People with Learning Disabilities and/or Autism Spectrum Disorder. Lancaster: Centre for Disability Research, Lancaster University. Accessed on 06/03/2019 at http://wp.lancs.ac.uk/cedr/files/2017/06/A-Trade-in-People-CeDR-2017-1.pdf

Buckland, R. (2014) 'The decision by Approved Mental Health Professionals to use compulsory powers under the Mental Health Act 1983: a Foucauldian discourse analysis.' *British Journal of Social Work 46*, 1, 46–62.

Care Quality Commission (2015) Housing with Care – Guidance on Regulated Activities for Providers of Supported Living and Extra Care Housing. Accessed on 06/03/2019 at www.cqc.org.uk/sites/default/files/20151023_provider_guidance-housing_with_care.pdf

CC v KK [2012] EWHC 2136 (COP), [2012] MHLO 89. Accessed on 04/03/2019 at www.bailii.org/ew/cases/EWCOP/2012/2136.html

CH v A Metropolitan Council [2017] EWCOP 12. Accessed on 04/03/2019 at http://www.bailii.org/ew/cases/EWCOP/2017/12.html

Clarke, C.L., Rhynas, S., Schwannauer, M. and Taylor, J. (2017) *Risk and Resilience: Global Learning across the Age Span*, Policy and Practice in Health and Social Care Number 24. Edinburgh: Dunedin Academic Press.

Commission for Healthcare Audit and Inspection (2006) Joint Investigation into the Provision of Services for People with Learning Disabilities at Cornwall Partnership NHS Trust. Accessed on 06/03/2019 at http://webarchive.nationalarchives.gov.uk/20080609161229/http://www.healthcarecommission.org.uk/_db/_documents/cornwall_investigation_report.pdf

Croisdale-Appleby, D. (2014) Re-visioning Social Work Education: An Independent Review. Accessed on 06/03/2019 at www.gov.uk/government/uploads/system/uploads/attachment_data/file/285788/DCA_Accessible.pdf

Davies, H.T.O., Nutley, S.M. and Mannion, R. (2000) 'Organisational culture and quality of health care.' *Quality and Safety in Health Care 9*, 2, 111–119.

Dawidowicz, L. (1976) *A Holocaust Reader*. Library of Jewish Studies. West Orange, NJ: Behrman House Inc.

Day, L. (2017) What are the Lessons from Veilstone? Accessed on 06/03/2019 at www.leighday.co.uk/Blog/June-2017/What-are-the-lessons-from-Veilstone.

Department for Constitutional Affairs (2013) *Mental Capacity Act 2005: Code of Practice*. London: HMSO

Department of Health and Social Care (2019) The Mental Capacity (Amendment) Bill. Accessed on 06/03/2019 at https://services.parliament.uk/bills/2017-19/mentalcapacityamendment.html

DH (Department of Health) (2008) Impact Assessment of the Mental Capacity Act Deprivation of Liberty Safeguards to Accompany the Code of Practice and Regulation. Accessed on 06/03/2019 at http://webarchive.nationalarchives. gov.uk/20130107105354/http:/www.dh.gov.uk/prod_consum_dh/groups/ dh_digitalassets/documents/digitalasset/dh_084984.pdf

Dominelli, L. (2009) *Introducing Social Work*. Cambridge: Polity Press.

EHRC (Equality and Human Rights Commission) (2016) Bournewood Case. Accessed on 15/07/2019 at www.equalityhumanrights.com/en/what-are-human-rights/human-rights-stories/bournewood-case

Emerson, E. and Hatton, C. (2008) People with Intellectual Disabilities in England. Research Report No. 2008 (1). Accessed on 06/03/2019 at www.lancaster.ac.uk/ staff/emersone/FASSWeb/Emerson_08_PWLDinEngland.pdf

Engel and Others v The Netherlands 5100/71 [1976] ECHR 3 (1976). Accessed on 24/10/2018 at http://hudoc.echr.coe.int/eng?i=001-57479#{"itemid":["001-57479"]}

Essex County Council v RF & Ors (Deprivation of Liberty and damage) [2015] EWCOP 1 (2015). Accessed on 15/07/2019 at www.bailii.org/ew/cases/ EWCOP/2015/1.html

Evans, C. (2015) Social Work Students Do Not Know What Makes a Difference to Service Users. Community Care, Accessed on 06/03/2019 at www. communitycare.co.uk/2015/05/26/social-work-students-know-makes-difference-service-users/

Ferguson, H. (2015) 'Researching social work practice close up: using ethnographic and mobile methods to understand encounters between social workers, children and families.' *British Journal of Social Work 46*, 153–168.

Ferguson, H. (2017) 'How children become invisible in child protection work: findings from research into day-to-day social work practice.' *The British Journal of Social Work 47*, 4, 1007–1023.

Flynn, M. (2012) South Gloucestershire Safeguarding Adults Board. Winterbourne View Hospital: A Serious Case Review. Accessed on 06/03/2019 at http:// hosted.southglos.gov.uk/wv/report.pdf

Flynn, M. (2018) *Safeguarding Adults Review Mendip House*. Somerset Safeguarding Adults Board. Accessed on 04/04/2019 at https://ssab.safeguardingsomerset. org.uk/wp-content/uploads/20180206_Mendip-House_SAR_FOR_ PUBLICATION.pdf

Fraser, N. and Honneth, A. (2003) *Redistribution or Recognition? A Political-Philosophical Exchange*. London: Verso.

Friedman, C. (2018) '"Every vote matters:" experiences of people with intellectual and developmental disabilities in the 2016 United States General Election.' *Review of Disability Studies 14*, 1.

Friedman, C. and Rizzolo, M. (2017) 'Correlates of voting participation of people with intellectual and developmental disabilities.' *Journal of Social Work in Disability and Rehabilitation 16*, 3–4, 347–360.

Garret, P. (2010) 'Recognizing the limitations of the political theory of recognition: Axel Honneth, Nancy Fraser and social work.' *British Journal of Social Work 40*, 5, 1517–1533.

Goodley, D. (2014) *Dis/Ability Studies: Theorising Disablism and Ableism*. Abingdon: Routledge.

Goodley, D. and Runswick-Cole, K. (2014) 'Becoming dis/human: thinking about the human through disability.' *Discourse: Studies in the Cultural Politics of Education.* DOI: 10.1080/01596306.2014.930021

Graeber, D. (2015) *The Utopia of Rules: On Technology, Stupidity, and the Secret Joys of Bureaucracy.* Brooklyn, NY: Meville House.

Guzzardi v Italy 7367/76 [1980] ECHR 5 (1980). Accessed on 04/03/2019 at www.bailii.org/eu/cases/ECHR/1980/5.html

Hatton C., Glover G., Emerson E. and Brown, I. (2016) *People with Learning Disabilities in England 2015.* London: Public Health England.

HSCIC (Health and Social Care Information Centre) (2013) Mental Capacity Act 2005, Deprivation of Liberty Safeguards (England), Annual Report 2012-13. Accessed on 03/11/2018 at https://digital.nhs.uk/data-and-information/publications/statistical/mental-capacity-act-2005-deprivation-of-liberty-safeguards-assessments

Hegel, M. (1977 [1807]) *The Phenomenology of Spirit.* Trans. A.V. Miller. Oxford: Galaxy Books, Oxford University Press.

Hendry, L.B. and Kloep, M. (2002) *Lifespan Development: Resources, Challenges and Risks: Resources, Challenges and Risks.* London: Thomson Learning.

Herzberg, F. (1959) *Motivation to Work.* New York: John Wiley & Sons.

HL v The United Kingdom 45508/99 [2004] ECHR 471, accessed on 11/07/2019 at www.bailii.org/eu/cases/ECHR/2004/471.html

Hood, I. (2016) 'It's our Scotland just as much as anyone else's.' *Tizard Intellectual Disability Review 21,* 1, 2–9.

Ife, J. (2008) *Human Rights and Social Work: Towards Rights-Based Practice,* second edition. New York: Cambridge University Press.

IFSW (International Federation of Social Workers) (2014) Global Definition of Social Work. Accessed on 04/04/2019 at www.ifsw.org/what-is-social-work/global-definition-of-social-work/

James, E. (2016) 'Participation of adults with intellectual disabilities in the UK 2015 General Election.' *York Policy Review 3.* Accessed on 06/03/2019 at http://yorkpolicyreview.co.uk/journalsite/volume-three/participation-of-adults-with-intellectual-disabilities-in-the-uk-2015-general-election/

James, E., Harvey, M. and Mitchell, R. (2017) 'The Mental Capacity Act call to action: online development of critical rights-based social work.' *Practice: Social Work in Action 29,* 4, 279–292.

James, E., Harvey, M. and Hatton, C. (2018) 'Learning disabled adults participation in the United Kingdom 2015 General Election.' *Tizard Learning Disability Review 23,* 2, 65–71.

James, E., Morgan, H. and Mitchell, R. (2017) 'Named social workers – better social work for learning disabled people?' *Disability & Society 32,* 10, 1650–1655.

Julian, G. (2015) Thoughts on Being Human... Or think before you speak/tweet #JusticeforLB. Accessed on 06/03/2019 at www.georgejulian.co.uk/2015/05/20/thoughts-on-being-human-or-think-before-you-speaktweet-justiceforlb/

Keane, F. (2015) Election Essay: What's love got to do with politics? Accessed on 09/07/2019 at www.bbc.co.uk/news/magazine-31610050

Keeley, H., Redley M., Holland, A.J. and Clare, I.C.H. (2008) 'Participation in the 2005 General Election by adults with intellectual disabilities.' *Journal of Intellectual Disability Research 52,* 3, 175–181.

Kinney, M. (2009) 'Being assessed under the 1983 Mental Health Act: can it ever be ethical?' *Ethics and Social Welfare 3,* 3, 329–336

Kjellberg, A. and Hemmingsson, H. (2013) 'Citizenship and voting: experiences of persons with intellectual disabilities in Sweden.' *Journal of Policy and Practice in Intellectual Disabilities 10*, 4, 326–333.

Law Commission (2015) *Mental Capacity and the Deprivation of Liberty: A Consultation Paper.* Consultation Paper No 222. Crown Copyright. Accessed on 09/07/2019 at www.lawcom.gov.uk/app/uploads/2015/07/cp222_mental_capacity.pdf

Law Commission (2017) *Mental Capacity and the Deprivation of Liberty.* Crown Copyright. Accessed on 04/03/2019 at www.lawcom.gov.uk/app/uploads/2017/03/lc372_mental_capacity.pdf

Lawler, J. and Bilson, A. (2010) *Social Work Management and Leadership.* London: Routledge.

Liddard, K. (2018) *The Intimate Lives of Disabled People.* Abingdon: Routledge.

Lipsky, M. (2010) *Street-level Bureaucracy: Dilemmas of the Individual in Public Services.* New York: Russell Sage Foundation.

Local Authority X v MM & Anor (No. 1) [2007] EWHC 2003 (Fam). Accessed on 04/03/2019 at www.bailii.org/ew/cases/EWHC/Fam/2007/2689.html

London Borough of Hillingdon v Neary & Anor [2011] EWCOP 1377 (2011). Accessed on 20.06.2017 at http://www.bailii.org/ew/cases/EWHC/COP/2011/1377.html

Lord, J.E., Ashley Stein, M. and Fiala-Butora, J. (2014) 'Facilitating an equal right to vote for persons with disabilities.' *Journal of Human Rights Practice 6*, 1, 115–139.

Magna Carta (1215) Accessed on 06/03/2019 at www.bl.uk/magna-carta/articles/magna-carta-english-translation

Mainiero, L. (1994) 'On breaking the glass ceiling: the political seasoning of powerful women executives.' *Organisational Dynamics 22*, 4, 5–20.

Meek, L.V. (1988) 'Organisational culture: origins and weaknesses.' *Organisational Studies 9*, 453–473.

Ministry of Justice (1989) Representation of the People Act. Accessed on 06/03/2019 at www.legislation.gov.uk/ukpga/1983/2

Ministry of Justice (1998) The Human Rights Act 1998. Accessed on 06/03/2019 at www.legislation.gov.uk/ukpga/1998/42/content

Ministry of Justice (2000) Representation of the People Act. Accessed on 06/03/2019 at www.legislation.gov.uk/ukpga/2000/2/contents

Ministry of Justice (2005) Mental Capacity Act. Accessed on 06/03/2019 at www.legislation.gov.uk/ukpga/2005/9/contents

Ministry of Justice (2006) Electoral Administration Act 2006. Accessed on 06/03/2019 at www.legislation.gov.uk/ukpga/2006/22/contents.

Morgan, H. (2012) 'The social model of disability as a threshold concept: troublesome knowledge and liminal spaces in social work education.' *Social Work Education 31*, 2, 215–226.

Morgan, H. and Roulstone, A. (2012) 'Editorial.' *Social Work Education 31*, 2, 137–141. https://doi.org/10.1080/02615479.2012.644941

Morris, J. (1993) *Independent Lives? Community Care and Disabled People.* Basingstoke: Palgrave.

Munby, L.J. (2011) 'Safeguarding and dignity: when is safeguarding abuse?' Keynote Address by Lord Justice Munby to the Rotherham, Doncaster and South Humber Mental Health NHS Foundation Trust's Approved Mental Health Professional and Social Care Conference.

Munro, E. (2011) The Munro review of child protection: a child-centred system. Accessed on 06/03/2019 at www.gov.uk/government/publications/munro-review-of-child-protection-final-report-a-child-centred-system

Neary, M. (2011) *Get Steven Home: The Story of a Year Long Battle to Enable a Young Autistic Man to Live at Home.* Morrisville, NC: Lulu Press, Inc.

New Economics Foundation (2012) Measuring Wellbeing – A Guide for Practitioners. Accessed on 06/03/2019 at https://neweconomics.org/uploads/files/8d92cf44e70b3d16e6_rgm6bpd3i.pdf

NHS Southern Health (2016) Trust Statement Regarding Connor Sparrowhawk's Death. Accessed on 04/04/2019 at www.southernhealth.nhs.uk/news-archive/2016/trust-statement-regarding-connor-sparrowhawks-death/

O'Donnell, P., Farrar, A., BrintzenhofeSzoc, K., Conrad, A.P. *et al.* (2008) 'Predictors of ethical stress, moral action and job satisfaction in health care social workers.' *Social Work Health Care 46*, 3, 29–51.

Oliver, M. (1990) *The Politics of Disablement: Critical Texts in Social Work and the Welfare State.* London: McMillan Education Ltd.

Oliver, M., Sapey, B. and Thomas, P. (2012) *Social Work with Disabled People*, 4th Edition. Basingstoke: Palgrave MacMillan.

Osgood, T. (2006) 'Still Hurting: What Jane Did Next.' Serviceland, Commissioning and Monitoring: A Triad of Impairments. Accessed on 03/09/2017 at https://kar.kent.ac.uk/33585/

P (by his litigation friend the Official Solicitor) *v Cheshire West and Chester Council & Anor*; and *P & Q* (by their litigation friend the Official Solicitor) *v Surrey County Council* [2014] UKSC 19. Accessed on 11/07/2019 at www.bailii.org/uk/cases/UKSC/2014/19.html

P v Surrey County Council & Surrey Downs CCG [2015] EWCOP 54. Accessed on 04/03/2019 at www.39essex.com/cop_cases/p-v-surrey-county-council-and-surrey-downs-ccg/

P & Q v Surrey County Council; sub nom Re MIG and MEG [2011] EWCA Civ 190. Accessed on 04/03/2019 at www.bailii.org/ew/cases/EWCA/Civ/2011/190.html

Percy Commission (1957) *Report of the Royal Commission on the Law Relating to Mental Illness and Mental Deficiency 1954–1957* (Cmnd 169). London: HMSO.

PH & A local authority v Z limited & R [2011] EWHC 1704. Accessed on 04/03/2019 at www.bailii.org/ew/cases/EWCOP/2011/1704.html.

Political and Constitutional Reform Committee (2014) Voter Engagement in the UK: Fourth Report of Session 2014–15. London: The Stationery Office.

Rautenbach, J.V. and Black-Hughes, C. (2012) 'Bridging the emispheres through the use of technology: international vollaboration in social work training.' *Journal of Social Work Education 48*, 797–815.

Re X (Court of Protection Practice) [2015] EWCA Civ 599, [2015] MHLO 44. Accessed on 04/03/2019 at www.bailii.org/ew/cases/EWCA/Civ/2015/599.html

Redley, M., Maina, E., Keeling, A. and Pattni, P. (2012) 'The voting rights of adults with intellectual disabilities: reflections on the arguments, and situation in Kenya and England and Wales.' *Journal of Intellectual Disability Research 56*, 11, 1026–1035.

Rochdale Metropolitan Borough Council v KW & Ors (Rev 1) [2014] EWCOP 45 (2014). Accessed on 04/03/2019 at www.bailii.org/ew/cases/EWCOP/2014/45.html

Ryan, S. (2018) *Justice for Laughing Boy: Connor Sparrowhawk - A Death by Indifference.* London: Jessica Kingsley Publishers.

Schein, E.H. (2004) *Organisational Culture and Leadership*, Third Edition. San Francisco, CA: Jossey-Bass.

Schön, D.A. (1983) *The Reflective Practitioner: How Professionals think in Action*. London: Ashgate.

Scott, T., Mannion, R., Davies, H and Marshall, M. (2003) 'The quantitative measurement of organizational culture in health care: a review of the available instruments.' *Health Services Research 38*, 3, 923–945.

Series, L. (2019) The Small Places. Accessed on 06/03/2019 at https://thesmallplaces.wordpress.com/

Sheffield City Council v E [2004] EWHC 2808 (Fam). Accessed on 10/01/2019, at www.bailii.org/ew/cases/EWHC/Fam/2004/2808.html

Socialist Health Association (2012) Ely Hospital Report. Accessed on 06/03/2019 at www.sochealth.co.uk/national-health-service/democracy-involvement-and-accountability-in-health/complaints-regulation-and-enquries/report-of-the-committee-of-inquiry-into-allegations-of-ill-treatment-of-patients-and-other-irregularities-at-the-ely-hospital-cardiff-1969/ely-hospital-report/

SR v A Local Authority [2018] EWCOP 36. Accessed on 04/03/2019 at www.bailii.org/ew/cases/EWCOP/2018/36.html

Stanev v Bulgaria [2012] ECHR 46. Accessed on 04/03/2019 at www.escr-net.org/sites/default/files/caselaw/decision_on_stanev_v._bulgaria_0.pdf

Steptoe, A., Deaton, A. and Stone A. (2014) 'Psychological wellbeing, health and aging.' *The Lancet 385*, 9968, 640–648.

Szerletics, A. (2012) Best interests decision-making under the Mental Capacity Act. Accessed on 06/03/2019 at http://autonomy.essex.ac.uk/best-interests-decision-making-under-the-mental-capacity-act

TCSW (The College of Social Work) (2012) The Business Case for Social Work with Adults: A Discussion Paper. Accessed on 06/03/2019 at http://cdn.basw.co.uk/upload/basw_100027-10.pdf

Turner, V.W. (1969) *The Ritual Process: Structure and Anti-Structure*. Chicago: Aldine Publishing Company.

UK Political Info (2016) General Election Turnout 1945–2015. Accessed on 06/03/2019 at www.ukpolitical.info/Turnout45.htm

United Nations (1948) Universal Declaration of Human Rights. Accessed on 06/03/2019 at www.un.org/en/universal-declaration-human-rights/index.html

United Nations (2006) Convention on the Rights of Persons with Disabilities. Accessed on 04/04/2019 at www.un.org/development/desa/disabilities/convention-on-the-rights-of-persons-with-disabilities/convention-on-the-rights-of-persons-with-disabilities-2.html

United Nations (undated) Human Rights Day. Accessed on 16/06/2019 at www.un.org/en/events/humanrightsday/

University of Sheffield (2018) iHuman. Accessed on 06/03/2019 at http://ihuman.group.shef.ac.uk/

Waitzkin, H. (1989) 'A critical theory of medical discourse: ideology, social control, and the processing of social context in medical encounters.' *Journal of Health and Social Behaviour 30*, 2, 220–239.

Webber Shandwick (2014) Employees Rising: Seizing the Opportunity in Employee Activism. Accessed on 02/04/2018 at www.webershandwick.com/uploads/news/files/employees-rising-seizing-the-opportunity-in-employee-activism.pdf

Werkmeister Rozas, L. and Garran, A.M. (2016) 'Towards a human rights culture in social work education.' *British Journal of Social Work 46*, 890–905.

Westminster City Council v Sykes [2014] EWCOP B9 (2014). Accessed on 22/11/2018 at www.bailii.org/ew/cases/EWHC/COP/2014/B9.html

Willis, D., McGlade, l., Gallagher, M. and Menabney, C. (2016) 'Voting and the Scottish referendum: perspectives of people with intellectual disabilities and their family and paid carers.' *Disability and Society 31*, 7, 914–928.

Winterwerp v The Netherlands [1979] ECHR 4. Accessed on 04/03/2019 at www.bailii.org/eu/cases/ECHR/1979/4.html

Wolfensberger, W. (1983) 'Social role valorization: a proposed new term for the principle of normalization.' *Mental Retardation 21*, 6, 234–239.

World Health Organization (2019) International Classification of Diseases. Accessed on 06/03/2019 at www.who.int/health-topics/international-classification-of-diseases.

Wye Valley NHS Trust v Mr B [2015] EWCOP 60. Accessed on 04/03/2019 at www.bailii.org/ew/cases/EWCOP/2015/60.html

Index